SHOWING

Whether or not wrongdoers show remorse and how ~~~~ ~~~ ers that attract great interest both in law and in popular culture. In capital trials in the United States, it can be a question of life or death whether a jury believes that a wrongdoer showed remorse. And in wrongdoings that capture the popular imagination, public attention focuses not only on the act but on whether the perpetrator feels remorse for what they did. But who decides when remorse should be shown or not shown, and whether it is genuine or not genuine? In contrast to previous academic studies on the subject, the primary focus of this work is not on whether the wrongdoer meets these expectations over how and when remorse should be shown, but on how the community reacts when these expectations are met or not met.

This book will be of interest to those in the fields of sociology, law, socio-legal studies, and criminology as well as to those readers with a general interest in the topic of remorse.

While contemporary criminal justice is officially secular and fact-driven, offenders are nevertheless expected to show remorse, and lack of visible remorse can have a marked negative impact in parole and probation contexts as well as in sentencing. In this innovative work, Richard Weisman explores the complex emotional, psychological, and legal issues raised by the criminal justice's system unwritten expectations about offending and remorse. The book will be of interest to criminologists, sociolegal scholars, forensic psychologists, defence lawyers, and judges, but it is also accessible to the general public.

Mariana Valverde, University of Toronto, Canada

For April

For Dan and Steve

Showing Remorse
Law and the Social Control of Emotion

RICHARD WEISMAN
York University, Canada

Routledge
Taylor & Francis Group

LONDON AND NEW YORK

First published 2014 by Ashgate Publishing

2 Park Square, Milton Park, Abingdon, Oxon OX14 4RN
711 Third Avenue, New York, NY 10017, USA

Routledge is an imprint of the Taylor & Francis Group, an informa business

First issued in paperback 2016

British Library Cataloguing in Publication Data
A catalogue record for this book is available from the British Library.

The Library of Congress has cataloged the printed edition as follows:
Weisman, Richard.
 Showing remorse : law and the social control of emotion / by Richard Weisman.
    pages cm. -- (Law, justice and power)
 Includes bibliographical references and index.
 ISBN 978-0-7546-7398-9 (hbk. : alk. paper) -- ISBN 978-0-7546-9123-5 (ebook) -- ISBN 978-1-4724-0302-5 (epub) 1. Law--Psychological aspects. 2. Remorse. I. Title.
 K346.W45 2014
 302.5'4--dc23

                                                                                            2013023953

ISBN 13: 978-0-7546-7398-9 (hbk)
ISBN 13: 978-1-138-26003-0 (pbk)

Contents

Acknowledgments

This project grew as a residue from my earlier research. Some 30 years ago, I had studied one of the most famous trials in American history—the Salem witchcraft trials of 1692—and what had remained memorable for me years later was not so much the moral panic that led to the execution of 19 innocent persons, as the efforts by those who participated in the hangings to undo the harm that had been caused. A decade later, I undertook to study an experiment involving psychiatric offenders who had been classified as psychopaths and after interviewing them and the persons who worked with them, I became aware how important it was to all who were involved whether those who had offended experienced remorse and how difficult it was to find agreement on the matter. When legal databases first became available in the middle 1990s, I began to explore how the term "remorse" was applied with a research tool far more powerful than any I had encountered before. The more places I looked, whether in law, in trials that captured the attention of the public, in news items, or in other public forums, the more I found. The result was a vertiginous experience that took me from wrongful convictions to crimes of obedience to societal shifts, such as what occurred in the Massachusetts Bay Colony in 1692, to the depiction of persons as monsters and as heroes, as well as to many other sites too numerous to mention. This book is the fruition of that long germinating process that began in the 1990s and even now I am left with many unanswered questions about a topic that still fascinates me.

A project of this length would simply have been impossible to sustain without the support of family, friends, as well as my colleagues and students at York University in Toronto. I am grateful for the continuing contact I have had in the past 20 years with the vibrant community of socio-legal scholars at my own university. The dialogue I have had with the serious young scholars in my graduate seminars on the Social Dimensions of Legal Discourse has been at least as enriching for me as hopefully it has been for my students. I must mention my former student and now professor Augustine Park for her work as research assistant for part of this project as well as her many thoughtful insights. Thanks to Austin Sarat for his support and encouragement to publish my research. I thank my dear colleagues in the Law and Society Program, especially Annie Bunting, Kimberley White, Jane McMillan, Allyson Lunny, and Dorathy Moore for their continuing appreciation and interest in my work and for presenting me with opportunities to share my ideas. I am indebted to Thomas, Joanne, Gabriel, and Paul for their openness in sharing the experiences they had in their encounters with the Canadian criminal justice system. I have been particularly fortunate to have the support of my friend and colleague, Justice David Cole of the Ontario Court of Justice, for his generosity, for his belief in and support for my research, and for his many helpful suggestions. My good friend and former student, Chris Adamson, sociologist, novelist, and short-story writer, has kindly read and offered wise and informed commentary on the manuscript—any blunders or awkward passages remain of course my responsibility. Chris and I have kept communion over the years on the joys and agonies of the creative process.

I owe the deepest of thanks to my family. In the time that it has taken for me to conceive of remorse as a researchable topic to the completion of this book, my sons, Dan and Steve, have grown from young boys to intelligent young adults—both have given me the priceless gift of goodwill and respect for my creative process. My partner, April, has given me the equally priceless gift of believing in me and in the value and importance of the project through the years it has taken to get to this point. It is to April, Dan, and Steve that I dedicate this book.

Chapter 1
Towards a Constructionist Approach to the Study of Remorse

In Albert Camus's classic novel, *The Outsider*, Meursault, the protagonist, is arrested and brought to court after he has shot and killed a man during an encounter on a beach. After a few exchanges in which the magistrate has become increasingly exasperated with Meursault, he asks him a final question: "Did (he) regret what (he) had done?" To which "after thinking a bit," (Meursault) replies that "what I felt was less regret than a kind of vexation—I couldn't find a better word for it (p. 74)."[1] The episode closes with the observation that after this exchange, "the magistrate seemed to have lost interest in me, and to have come to some sort of decision about my case (p. 75)." Just before he is sentenced to death, the prosecutor offers in his summation to the court other examples of Meursault's character: the day after his mother died, Meursault embarked on an affair and while at his mother's funeral, he lamented that he could have had a nice walk if only he hadn't been obliged to be present—evidence that, in the prosecutor's opinion, shows that Meursault was already a criminal at heart. But the most damning evidence is saved for last: "Has he so much as expressed any remorse? Never gentleman. Not once in the course of these proceedings did this man show the least contrition (p. 101)." Continuing his summation, the prosecutor declares, "This man has, I repeat, no place in a community whose basic principles he flouts without compunction. Nor, heartless as he is, has he any claim to mercy (p. 102)." Finally, the prosecutor concludes with this plea for the death penalty: "For if in the course of what has been a long career I have had occasion to call for the death penalty, never as strongly as today have I felt this painful duty made easier, lighter, clearer by the certain knowledge of a sacred imperative and by the horror I feel when I look into a man's face and see a monster (p. 104)."

I have chosen to begin my book with this famous passage not just for the obvious reason that it refers to the showing of remorse and is therefore a fitting introduction to a book dedicated to the subject. I begin with this excerpt because it is one of the very few among the many literary classics that touch upon remorse to have called attention to a part of the phenomenon that has either been ignored or unrecognized by everyone else.[2] And it is what Camus tells us about remorse

---

1   All quotes taken from Albert Camus, *The Stranger* (trans. Matthew Ward, Alfred Knopf, 1989).

2   The other most well-known exception is the passage in J.M. Coetzee's *Disgrace* (Secker and Warburg, 1999), in which the central character, David Lurie, is brought before

that likewise differentiates the present work from the vast array of academic works in moral philosophy, psychology, criminology, and sociology that have also laid claim to this topic.

As we read this passage about the response of a prosecutor in a French court in a work that was published some 70 years ago, there is nevertheless an unmistakable sense of familiarity with the setting even as we are separated by time and culture. If we identify ever so slightly with Meursault, there is a part of us that wishes that he were less honest about how he actually felt and that he show the judge and the prosecutor the feelings that we all know they expect. Because we can experience the dread of what is going to happen to Meursault when he does not show these feelings. For the crime of murder, Meursault will go to prison. But for his failure to show the emotions we expect from someone who has been convicted of murder, he will have to die. For not showing remorse, Meursault has become not merely a man who has committed a murder—he is now a monster whose life must be extinguished.

This impassioned and sobering response to Meursault's performance in court illustrates the central proposition of this work—namely, that feelings of remorse are subject to social regulation either through collective approval or, as in this case, collective condemnation. When I suggest that the following analysis takes a different direction to the showing of remorse from most of the academic work that has preceded it, it is because my focus is not primarily on the transgressor who has breached communal norms and from whom we expect a show of remorse, but rather on the community that imposes these norms.[3] It is the prosecutor and the judge rather than Meursault who are the protagonists in this work. My concern is not with the adequacy or inadequacy of Meursault's response to the expectation to show remorse but rather with the expectation itself and the meanings that the community attaches to whether or not these expectations are fulfilled.

More generally, my approach builds on and contributes to the corpus of research initiated in the pioneering efforts of Arlie Hochschild and others to make visible the centrality of emotions in social interaction through close observation of the ways in which feelings are managed by self and others. The conceptual tools that Hochschild developed with respect to the management of emotions in general are particularly well suited to the study of expressions of remorse. As an object of inquiry, the showing of remorse offers a rich opportunity for exploring what

---

an academic tribunal on charges of sexual harassment, refuses to show remorse, and as a result loses his job as a tenured professor.

3   Two recent exceptions to this generalization are Linda A. Wood and Clare McMartin, "Constructing Remorse: Judge's Sentencing Decisions in Child Sexual Assault," *Journal of Language and Social Psychology,* 2007, Vol. 26, no. 4, pp. 343–362 and Jennifer Kilty, "Gendering Violence, Remorse and the Role of Restorative Justice: Deconstructing Public Perceptions of Kelly Ellard and Warren Glotawski," *Contemporary Justice Review,* 2010, Vol. 13, no. 2, pp. 155–172. Both articles focus on the interpretations of those who categorize wrongdoers as remorseful or remorseless.

Hochschild has referred to as "feeling rules"[4] or those norms that communicate when it is appropriate or "right" to experience a feeling, how these feelings should be expressed, and how to distinguish between expressions that are genuine and those that are false. In the chapters below, I hope to show that these processes by which members decide when and how remorse should be expressed is one of the means by which we create, maintain, and transform the moral boundaries of society. As illustrated in the judicial response to Meursault, violations of the feeling rules for remorse are occasions for moral outrage—unwillingness or inability to conform to the feeling rules attached to remorse leaves the transgressor open to the charge of betrayal of community at what is perceived as the core of their character. It is another objective of this work to make sense of this passionate response in the contexts that I examine by making visible what is at stake in the crediting or discrediting of these public expressions of remorse for both the individual and the community.

But, before undertaking this analysis, I want to explain why I have chosen law as the primary site of inquiry from which to undertake this study, to specify the perspective from which I approach the showing of remorse building on earlier conceptualizations, and to outline the basis on which I organized the chapters to follow.

Law as a Site of Inquiry

It is fitting that Camus should have fixed upon the court as the ultimate moral arbiter of Meursault's character. For all their purported focus on the act rather than the person, the legal regimes to be considered below—Canadian, American, and South African, in particular—but others as well are remarkably concerned with questions of attitude, demeanor, and other attributes that reach inside the mind of the offender.[5] Prime among these considerations is whether or not those who have violated the legal and moral codes of their communities experience and express remorse.

The impact of this designation of persons as (remorseful or unremorseful) derives both from its scope—the extent of its use—and the multiple meanings attached to it in the different contexts in which it as applied. It has been recognized for some time, although the phenomenon is still surprisingly under-researched and

---

4   For elaboration of this concept, see Arlie Hochschild, *The Commercialization of Intimate Life: Notes from Home and Work*, University of California Press, 2001, pp. 99–103.

5   For example, among the major works of the last 15 years that have looked at the mobilization of shame and disgust in the law, see Martha C. Nussbaum, *Hiding From Humanity: Disgust, Shame, and the Law*, Princeton University Press, 2004; Susan Bandes, ed., *The Passions of the Law*, New York University Press, 1999, see especially contributions of Nussbaum, Dan Kahan; and, more generally, William Ian Miller, *The Anatomy of Disgust*, Harvard University Press, 1998.

explored, that attributions of remorse play an important role in decisions affecting sentencing, bail, and parole in both Canada and the United States.[6] Indeed, recent scholarship has suggested that similar concerns about demeanor are to be found in such disparate legal cultures as that of Japan, China, Sweden, and the Netherlands.[7] Moreover, it is clear that considerations of remorse have been incorporated in the newly emerging legal forums of international criminal law, such as International War Crimes Tribunals and Truth Commissions.[8]

But, perhaps there is no line of research more cogent than the enormously prolific U.S. National Capital Jury Project in demonstrating both the weight and gravity accorded to attributions of remorse. Numerous articles emanating from this project, which began in 1993 using a sample of 1,155 real jurors from 340 capital trials in 14 states, have attested to the crucial importance that jurors attach to the offender's show of remorse in deciding whether or not to impose the death penalty. In one of these studies involving California jurors in 37 capital cases, for example, it was found that 69 percent of jurors who voted for death in the bifurcated, penalty phase of the capital trial cited remorse as the principal factor in their decision.[9] Another finding from the same study showed that in all the cases in which juries voted for life, there was at least one juror who believed that offender

6   Michael Proeve and Steven Tudor's book, *Remorse: Psychological and Jurisprudential Perspectives,* Ashgate, 2010, is one of the very few recent works to have begun to fill this void.

7   See especially, Yanrong Chang, *Culture and Communication: An Ethnographic Study of Chinese Courtroom Communications* (PhD thesis, University of Iowa, 2001) [unpublished]; David T. Johnson, *The Japanese Way of Justice: Prosecuting Crime in Japan,* New York: Oxford University Press, 2002; Leif Dahlberg, "Emotional Tropes in the Courtroom: On Representation of Affect and Emotion in Legal Court Proceedings," *Nordic Theater Studies,* 2009, Vol. 21, pp. 129–152; and Martha Komter, *Dilemmas in the Courtroom: A study of the trials of violent crime in the Netherlands,* Erlbaum Associates: New Jersey, 1998 for discussions of the role of remorse in criminal justice systems in China, Japan, Sweden, and Netherlands, respectively.

8   See Tim Kelsall, "Truth, Lies, and Ritual: Preliminary Reflections on the Truth and Reconciliation Commission in Sierra Leone," *Human Rights Quarterly 27,* 2005, pp. 361–391; Richard Weisman, "Showing Remorse at the TRC: Towards a Constitutive Approach to Reparative Justice," *University of Windsor Annual Review—Access to Justice,* 2006, Vol. 24, no. 2, "Special Issue on Problems Concerning Human Rights," Vol. 24, no. 2, pp. 221–239; Leigh A. Payne, *Unsettling Accounts: Neither Truth Nor Reconciliation in Confessions of State Violence,* Durham, N.C., Duke University Press, 2008, see especially Chapter 2 entitled "Remorse."

9   Scott Sundby, "Symposium: The Capital Jury and Absolution: The Intersection of Trial Strategy, Remorse, and the Death Penalty," 83 *Cornell L.R.,* 1998, pp. 1557–1598; see also the other most frequented cited article from the study on this topic, Theodore Eisenberg, Stephen P. Garvey, and Martin T. Wells, "But Was He Sorry? The Role of Remorse in Capital Sentencing, 83 *Cornell L.R.,* 1998, pp. 1599–1637. As one of the jurors stated in Sundby's account of a capital trial in which the jury voted for the death penalty, "I think if he had shown any remorse, if he had started crying, it would have been all over, we

might have been remorseful. These findings corroborate the earlier research of Costanza and Peterson who, almost in reprise to Camus's fictional account, studied summary addresses by prosecutors to capital juries and determined that one of the most recurrent themes was the remorselessness of the offender and concluded that "wherever possible, prosecutors emphasized the offender's apparent lack of remorse."[10] The National Capital Jury project would seem to confirm the aptness of this prosecutorial strategy for mobilizing public sentiment.

But the extraordinary impact of this attribution has not gone unnoticed even within the legal forum itself. When there is so much at stake in whether or not remorse is present, it should not be surprising that the process by which expressions of remorse are validated or invalidated has been the subject of frequent and intense legal contestation. A search on LexisNexis reveals close to 1,700 legal actions in capital cases in the United States between 1990 and 2010, in which the convicted person's remorsefulness or its absence is mentioned at least three times.[11] Perhaps the most conspicuous judicial acknowledgment of the crucial role of remorse in death penalty decisions occurred in the U.S. Supreme Court decision of 1992, *Riggins v. Nevada*.[12] In this case, a man who had been sentenced to death was allowed a retrial on grounds that the medication he received for his depression may have hampered his ability to express remorse. As Justice Anthony Kennedy observed in a concurring opinion, "... as any trial attorney can attest, serious prejudice could result if medication inhibits the defendant's capacity to react to proceedings and to demonstrate remorse or compassion. The prejudice can be acute during the sentencing phase of the proceedings, when the sentencers must attempt to know the heart and mind of the offender."[13] More recently, another U.S. Supreme Court judgment held that persons who fell into the category of the "mentally retarded" would heretofore be exempted from the death penalty in part because such defendants "are typically poor witnesses, and their demeanor may create an unwarranted impression of lack of remorse for their crimes."[14] The

---

never could have voted for death," Sundby, *A Life and Death Decision: A Jury Weighs the Death Penalty*, Palgrave Macmillan, New York, 2005, p. 33.

10   Mark Costanzo and Julie Peterson, "Attorney Persuasion in the Capital Penalty Phase: A content Analysis of Closing Arguments," *J. of Social Issues*, Summer, 1994, p. 125. A more recent analysis of capital cases drawing from the Capital Jury study shows how this strategy is used by prosecutors in capital jury cases in Texas—see Elizabeth S. Vartkessian, "Dangerously Biased: How the Texas Capital Sentencing Statute Encourages Jurors to be Unreceptive to Mitigation Evidence," 29 Quinnipiac Law Review, 2011, p. 270.

11   Data retrieved from LexisNexis on February 10, 2013. I began with 1990 as the date by which a substantial jurisprudence on capital cases had accumulated.. Under US Legal, I entered the search terms "death penalty" and "atleast3remors!" to compile the number of individual judgments in which these terms were mentioned in the 20 year period between January 1, 1990 and December 31, 2010. Some 1,690 cases were so identified.

12   *Riggins v. Nevada* [1992] 112 U.S. Supreme Ct., p. 1810.

13   ibid, p. 1824.

14   *Atkins v. Virginia* [2002] 112 U.S. Supreme Ct., p. 2252.

substantial impact of characterizations of the offender as remorseful or not to judicial outcomes has been quietly, if selectively, acknowledged within U.S. law for some time and is now amply supported by recent empirical investigation.

Yet it is the ubiquity of remorse in legal decision-making, even more than its sensational manifestations in capital trials, that recommends law as a strategic point of entry into the study of how moral emotions are socially regulated.

Each of the major philosophies of punishment with which the coercive power of the state is justified incorporate expressions of remorse albeit in somewhat different forms. Retributive approaches whether expressed as just deserts or in the language of distributive justice or in the language of atonement speak of remorse as a form of suffering that the perpetrator deserves to endure by virtue of the harm done to the victim.[15] In the moral economy of retributive penology, the pain and suffering which results from remorse can be discounted from the deprivations wrought by punishment. In Chapter 2, we shall have occasion to consider how these expectations that the intensity of emotional suffering be roughly commensurate with the harm done influence judicial evaluations of whether or not the offender's show of remorse is genuine. The more dominant penal philosophy in Canadian and American judicial discourse, however, is deterrence theory, and it is in accordance with the terms of this theory that courts and parole boards are most likely to justify their insistence on expressions of remorse. From the standpoint of deterrence theory, mitigation and other reductions in punishment as a result of remorse are justified because, it is argued, remorseful offenders are less likely to reoffend. Deterrence theory suggests that persons who show remorse have acquired the inner emotional controls that are the most reliable preventatives against anti-social conduct since the person is inhibited not by fear of the consequences, which is occasional at best, but by conscience which is purportedly rooted in the person's core personality. It is because of widespread belief[16] that there is such a correlation

---

15   I have grouped these approaches together because all of them view remorse as important, not because it may be instrumental in preventing further wrongdoing but because it is a form of suffering that is itself part of the punishment and justifiably so. For articles that describe or advocate this approach, see Stephen Garvey, "Punishment as Atonement" 46, UCLA Law Review (1999), 1814, and Linda Ross Meyer, "Eternal Remorse," in *Towards a Critique of Guilt: Perspective from the Law and the Humanities, Studies in Law, Politics, and Society* (2005), Vol. 36, pp. 139–154. For additional commentary on retributive approach, see Jeffrie Murphy, "Remorse, Apology, and Mercy," 4 *Ohio J. of Criminal Law* (2007), pp. 423–454.

16   I use the term "belief" advisedly. While it is not the purpose of this book to challenge or defend the proposition that remorse is correlated with recidivism—that persons who are credited with remorse are less likely to reoffend—it should be acknowledged that it is an assertion that has come under attack on two principal grounds. The first ground is that there is no empirical evidence to support this proposition: see, for example Mirko Bajaric and Kumar Amarkkehara, "Feeling Sorry? Tell Someone Who Cares: The Uselessness of Remorse in Sentencing," (2001) *Howard Journal* 40: 364–376. See also Michael M. O'Hear, "Appelate Review of Sentences: Reconsidering Differences," (2010) 51 Wm. and

between remorse and recidivism that decisions about sentencing and parole are likely to also involve judgments about remorse. In Chapter 4, I have tried to make more visible the enforcement of these "feeling rules" by courts and parole boards by looking at the official response to persons who refuse to show remorse because of principled objection to a norm or because they have been wrongfully convicted.

More recent approaches to criminal justice that are grouped under the rubric of restorative justice and that stress the restoration of ruptured relationships as the goal of state intervention also tend to require a demonstration of remorse as a precondition for any dialogue between offender and victim.[17] In Chapter 5, I will explore such a regime through an analysis of how public demonstrations of remorse were incorporated into the Truth and Reconciliation Commission hearings in South Africa from 1996–2000. My purpose in that chapter is to analyze the link between individual expressions of remorse and social transformation—how agreement with or resistance to the social expectation to show remorse came to embody the deeper social and ideological divisions in South African society.

Beyond these historical and jurisprudential roots in legal discourse, considerations of remorse that originate in the legal domain are also evident in that part of the official crime narrative that is most easily translated into popular discourse. Whether it is the perpetrator of atrocities committed in the name of the state or those who have committed the most notorious and heinous of crimes, it is often the ascription of remorse to the offender even more than their transgression that commands the attention of the courts and the public.

When Timothy McVeigh was executed on June 12, 2001 for the bombing of the Murrah Federal Building in Oklahoma City on April 19, 1995 that resulted in 168 deaths and wounded hundreds of others, it was not his death or his crime but rather his demeanor that became the focal point of public discussion. Typical among the headlines were "McVeigh Shows No Remorse" or "Death of a Terrorist

---

Mary L. Rev., 2123, who comments that there is "very little research to substantiate the claim that expressions of remorse predict reduced recidivism." The second ground of attack argues that, even if there were such a correlation, it is not possible to reliably distinguish true from manufactured feelings of remorse: see, for example, Brian Ward, "Sentencing Without Remorse," (2006) *Loy. U. Chi. L.J.* 38: 137–167. For contemporary defense of principle of mitigation for remorseful offenders, see Steven Tudor, "Why Should Remorse Be a Mitigating Factor in Sentencing?" (2008) *Criminal Law and Philosophy* Vol. 2, no. 3, pp. 241–257. See also Michael Proeve and Steven Tudor, "Remorse as a Mitigating Factor in Sentencing," pp. 115–138 in Michael Proeve and Steven Tudor, *Remorse: Psychological and Jurisprudential Perspectives*, Ashgate Press, 2010. Tudor's defense of the principle rests less on whether there is empirical support for the proposition than on the premise that remorse is a moral good that should be recognized and that one expression of this recognition is a reduced sentence.

17　See Allison Morris, "Shame, Guilt, and Remorse: Experiences from Family Group Conferences in New Zealand" in Ido Weijers and Antony Duff, eds, *Punishing Juveniles: Principle and Critique*, Portland, Oregon: Hart Publishing, 2002, 157 for discussion of central role of remorse in restorative justice mediations.

Last Rites Renew Issue of Remorse" or "Without Remorse McVeigh Put to Death" or "McVeigh executed for Oklahoma Site Bombing: Dies with no Trace of Remorse."[18] The court's subjection of offenders to moral ordering in terms of the presence or absence of remorse is amplified in public discourse into a drama of redemption and re-inclusion for those credited with remorse and dehumanization and moral outrage for those who are not.[19]

It is for these reasons that I have chosen legal discourse as my primary site for inquiring into the social processes by which remorse is attributed, the meanings that these attributions have for those to whom they are applied, and the impact of these judgments on the community as a whole. Courtrooms and tribunals as well as the ancillary institutions to which they are attached are among the key reality-defining institutions of modern society. It matters how courts and correctional facilities define remorse, how they ascribe moral character, how they decide which expressions of remorse are valid and which are not, and what consequences they attach to these assessments. That it is through attributions of remorse that courts create moral hierarchies among offenders and that so much is at stake in how these inner feelings are interpreted makes the process not just an occasion for affirming communal values but also a site of potential conflict between rival opinions of whether remorse has been demonstrated or even whether remorse should be demonstrated. As we shall see in the differing contexts examined in this book— Canadian, American, and South African—the imputation of remorse is marked by negotiation, contestation, surrender and opposition, claims and counterclaims, and power and resistance.

But, first, it is necessary to define more precisely the vantage point from which the showing of remorse will be approached in the chapters that follow.

Showing Remorse as a Social Practice

Remorse and Apology

In the following chapters, I approach remorse not as a feeling as it is experienced by an individual in isolation but rather as a communication to an audience. It is how

---

18   I generated a population of 275 news items by using *Factiva* to search for all news publications for articles that mentioned Timothy McVeigh and remorse between June 10 and June 14, 2001. The headlines I cited are respectively, Kevin Fagan, "McVeigh Shows No Remorse," *San Francisco Chronicle*, June 11, 2001, p. A1; Dan Herbeck and Lou Michel, "Death of a Terrorist Last Rites Renew Issue of Remorse," *Buffalo News*, June 12, 2001, p. A1; Lois Romano, " Without Remorse McVeigh Put to Death," *Virginia Pilot and the Ledger-Star*, June 12, p. A11; and Rex W. Huppke, "McVeigh Executed for Oklahoma Site Bombing: Dies With No Trace of Remorse," *Associated Press Newswire*.

19   See Austin Sarat, "Remorse, Responsibility, and Criminal Punishment: An Analysis of Popular Culture," in Bandes, ed. *Passions of the Law*, pp. 168–190.

remorse is shown and perceived rather than the feeling of remorse that will be the object of this inquiry. In adopting this focus, I am building on Erving Goffman's useful formulation of the offering of an apology or the showing of remorse as remedial exchanges. According to Goffman, in both forms of communication, the wrongdoer virtually splits herself or himself between the self that committed the offense and the self that joins with the aggrieved party in agreeing that the act was morally unacceptable.[20] The work of expressing remorse or the offering of apology—if believed—is to represent the wrongdoer as not aligned with the act for which she or he has been condemned. If the apology or the showing of remorse is successful, then it may be inferred that the self that *condemned* the act is more real than the self that committed the act. Contrariwise, for those who are viewed as unapologetic or unremorseful, the act becomes their essence. If they do not separate themselves from the act or if their apology or show of remorse is not believed, then the transgression comes to define who they are—the self that committed the offending act is the true self. Building on Goffman's formulation, we can conceive of the making of an apology or the showing of remorse as rituals in which the wrongdoer seeks to establish that their being—who they truly are— is different from their doing- their committing of the wrong that gave offense to a victim. These exchanges are remedial, according to Goffman, because they can result in reconciliation between the person who committed the wrong and the person who was injured by the wrong.

But I also want to suggest that the terminology used in legal discourse in which what is claimed, scrutinized, and contested is the showing of remorse rather than the offering of apology is not accidental. While there are important areas of overlap between apology and remorse, there are equally significant differences that make the social practices involved in the shaping of remorse distinct from those involved in the offering of apology. Indeed, if Murray Cox's lament in his posthumously edited collection, *Remorse and Reparation,* in 1999 still holds true in 2013, that despite the ubiquity of remorse in law and social relationships—"it pops up here and there"—and despite its crossing of disciplinary boundaries, there are still surprisingly few major works in any field in which remorse is the "predominant theme,"[21] one possible reason for this lacuna is that remorse has already been assimilated into analyses of the closely related phenomenon of apology. With a few notable exceptions, the scholarly literature has tended to view remorse as synonymous with apology—as if offering an apology was both functionally and semiotically equivalent to the showing of remorse—or as if remorse were an integral and inseparable component of the ritual of apology.[22]

---

20   Erving Goffman, *Relations in Public,* New York: Basic Books, 1972, p. 113.

21   Murray Cox, ed., *Remorse and Reparation,* Jessica Kingsley Publishers, 1999, p. 13. Exceptions are Proeve and Tudor (see n 4) and Steven Tudor's, *Compassion and Remorse*, Leuven, 2001.

22   The literature on the subject is divided, albeit inadvertently, over whether the apology and remorse are conceptually distinct, with the major sociological theorists merging

What distinguishes the showing of remorse from the offering of apology is how the separation between self and act is communicated. Here is where the differences become more significant than the similarities. While an apology may refer to the anguish and pain that the offender feels at having contravened the norms of the community, an expression of remorse shows or demonstrates this pain by making the suffering visible. Conventional usages in law and psychiatry describe remorse as an emotion that is shown rather than spoken: they typically refer to or discuss it in terms of "signs", "symptoms", "manifestations" or "demonstrations."[23] What this suggests is that remorse is communicated through gestures, displays of affect, and other paralinguistic devices rather than only through words. Both the apology and the expression of remorse can be communicated through simple linguistic formulae such as "I am sorry." With the former, however, we are likely to attend to the words; with the latter, we focus on how the words are expressed or the feelings that accompany the words. It was exactly in this sense that the lawyers for Riggins challenged his death sentence—because as they wrote—"the medication he was compelled to ingest dramatically altered Riggins' appearance before the jury. Instead of seeing a man who was concerned and nervous about his fate and remorseful for his actions, the jury was presented with a man who appeared cold, apathetic, and without remorse."[24] The effect of the medication was that Riggins could not through his demeanor make his suffering visible to the jury and was thus unable to show remorse. In showing remorse, one shows on one's body the power of community—the person who gave offense gives the other access to the private self—the self that is withheld from public view. In the process, what is revealed

the two—see *infra* notes 13 and 14—while other scholars make a clear separation—see Antony Duff, *Punishment, Communication, and Community*, New York: Oxford University Press, 2001, at 95, and Sharon Lamb, "Symposium: Responsibility and Blame: Psychological and Legal Perspectives" (2003*), Brooklyn L. R.* 929 at 954–955. As of this writing, the two most recent extended academic treatises on apology, Nick Young's *I was Wrong: The Meanings of Apologies,* Cambridge University Press, 2008, and Christopher Bennett, *The Apology Ritual: A Philosophical Theory of Punishment*, Cambridge University Press, 2008, continue the practice of subsuming the showing of remorse under apology or of simply not recognizing the showing of remorse as a phenomenon distinct from apology. Proeve and Tudor, see n. 4, the most recent contributors to this literature, subsume the offering of apology within the showing of remorse, viewing apology as "a behavioral aspect of remorse available in the shorter term." p. 74.

23   For psychiatric usage see, for example, the language used to describe the showing of remorse in E. Mark Stern, ed., *Psychotherapy and the Remorseful Patient*, Haworth Press, 1989, in a work in which therapists discuss the role of remorse in therapy—and its manifestation as symptoms—see especially James Dublin, "Remorse as Mental Dyspepsia," pp. 161–174 and Peter Shabad, "Remorse: The Echo of Inner Truth," pp. 113–133.

24   *David Riggins, Petitioner v. State of Nevada, Respondent* [1990] U.S. Briefs 8466, p. 16.

is that the private self as well as the public self has been touched by the values of community.[25]

This representational quality of remorse is allied with another element that further demarcates its expression from that of the apology. Feelings of remorse are expected to be painful, unwanted, and spontaneous rather than deliberate or planned. That demonstrations of remorse are often described as "breaking down" or "losing control", or as symptomatic of emotional collapse, fits well with their perceived involuntary character. It is illustrative of this usage that the jurors in the National Jury Project found awkward self-presentations more credible as expressions of remorse than presentations that were more competent or controlled or that popular usages will typically refer to such paralinguistic cues as tears or broken speech as evidence of remorse.[26] This emphasis on the non-verbal component of remorse is evident as well in those who are judged as lacking in remorse. Just as the flooding out of uncontrolled emotions can be read as a sign of remorse, so can the absence of any visible physical or psychological discomfort be read as the absence of remorse. Timothy McVeigh's choice to remain mute at his execution—or "stone-faced",[27] as several reporters described him— was read by most observers not as an abstention from the demand to show remorse but as a clear expression of a lack of remorse. As we shall see, in the public spaces of the court or the tribunals that we shall consider, there is no such thing as a non-performance. Silence is as meaningful as demonstrativeness and just as consequential in its legal and public repercussions.

Legal and popular discourses privilege the showing of remorse over the offering of apology. Feelings of remorse or their absence are perceived as reflecting core attributes of the person who has offended. While an apology may convey in words meanings that are fully consistent with what is expressed in the showing of remorse, contemporary usage accords greater weight to feelings than to words. How a person feels is perceived as revealing a truth that words alone cannot achieve. It is this crucial assumption, that a show of remorse reflects the essence of the person, that helps explain its use by judges and forensic psychologists as a predictor of future behavior, its impact on capital case jurors in deciding whether the offender who has murdered is to be defined by his actions or his feelings about his actions, and its power to mobilize the public in sympathy with or in condemnation of the person who has transgressed.

---

25 As Thomas Moore has put it, "remorse gives outer behavior interiority." See Moore, "Re-Morse: An Initiatory Disturbance of the Soul," in Stern, *Psychotherapy and the Remorseful Patient*, p. 84.

26 For National Capital Jury Project, see Sundby, *op. cit.*, pp. 1564–1565.

27 Kevin Fagan and Chuck Squatrigila, "Death of a Terrorist: McVeigh Offers No Last Words, Only a Steely Stare for His Victims," *San Francisco Chronicle*, June 12, 2001, p. A1. Also Karen Abbott, "Witness: 'It's Over' Timothy McVeigh has no Last Words but Stares Straight into Camera Before Dying," *Rocky Mountain News*, June 12, 2001, p. 2A.

Yet, paradoxically, it is this same belief in the authenticity of expressions of remorse that makes the process of validation so volatile a site of conflict in both legal and popular discourse. Because feelings of remorse are expected to originate from inner experience, beyond the realm of appearances, any artifice, dramaturgy, or other effort at the management of impressions is enough to dispel our suspension of disbelief that what is shown corresponds to what is felt. This potential gap between reality and appearance is amplified in the context of law. Where so much is at stake in deciding whether or not an expression of remorse can be credited as real, there is a continuing suspicion that what is demonstrated may be strategic rather than authentic, motivated by the promise of reward or leniency rather than by genuine inner feelings. Even those demonstrations that appear most convincing can be subject to retrospective interpretation as spurious and unconvincing as are those moral performances that appear least convincing also subject to contestation. For every claim that a wrongdoer feels and has demonstrated genuine remorse, there is a counterclaim that what purports to be spontaneous and real is belied by a desire to reap the benefits attached to it or to avoid the more dire consequences when remorse is judged to be absent. Indeed, this gap between appearance and reality can also work the other way. Just as a claim to be remorseful can be invalidated by an unconvincing display of feeling or by actions that are viewed as inconsistent with these claims, so can a claim not to feel remorse also be challenged by what are perceived as underlying feelings of guilt. A few of the witnesses to McVeigh's execution claimed to have discerned signs of tension and stress in his manner as if his body were revealing a truth at variance with his apparent composure.[28]

In the showing of remorse, we are left with a troubling question that pervades all such public demonstrations of feeling—how much of what is shown is a true expression of feeling and how much is intended to produce an effect on the audience? Especially on those occasions where victim and offender have a great stake in this perception of congruence between inner feeling and outer display, such expressions can become sites of contestation over whether these feelings are genuine or feigned, spontaneous or strategic, or deeply felt or superficial. How these contests are decided and by whom will be one of the central concerns of this work.

Remorse and Membership in the Moral Community

But there is another dimension to the showing of remorse that goes beyond the interchange between the wrongdoer and the victim or between the wrongdoer and the state. Here I draw upon the valuable work of Nicholas Tavuchis who postulated

---

28 For example, Grace BradBerry, "Victims' Families Come Face to Face with Killer—McVeigh Execution," *The Times,* June 12, 2001, p. 4, reports that one witness "saw his jaw quiver", while another said he saw "a little bit of sorrow. His chin did look like he was wanting to cry."

in his formulation of the ritual of apology that the "apology speaks to something larger than any particular offense and works its magic by a kind of speech that cannot be contained or understood merely in terms of expediency or the desire to achieve reconciliation."[29]

Tavuchis's important insight was to recognize that there is an inextricable moral component to these rituals that cannot be reduced to their instrumental functions as forms of social or remedial exchange. It is through these rituals that members define, negotiate, and transform what Tavuchis refers to as the moral community—or those agreed upon informal or formal rules the violation of which obliges members to offer an apology or to feel and express remorse. To approve or disapprove of any apology or a show of remorse is not merely an act of enforcement just as to offer an apology or to show remorse is not merely an act of compliance with the expectations of a moral community. The apology that is accepted or the show of remorse that is believed, are not just acts that may reconcile victim and wrongdoer—they are also acts by which the wrongdoer re-establishes their membership in the moral community. To fail to apologize when an apology is expected or to lack remorse where feelings of remorse are expected is to demonstrate that one does not belong to this moral community whether through defiance as many interpreted McVeigh's silence at his execution or through an incapacity to feel the way one is supposed to feel as perhaps could be attributed to Meursault.

Moral communities exert pressure on their members both to show remorse and not to show remorse. Prohibitions against the expression of remorse are likely to be most explicit when persons are recruited or conscripted into institutions or groups whose purposes and practices are antithetical to the groups with which they were previously affiliated. Studies and descriptions of military training for war offer rich illustrations of the social processes by which new recruits learn to overcome moral inhibitions towards killing. Indeed, some of the most famous speeches during World War II may be taken as applauding as heroic the very acts that in civilian contexts would have called for public expressions of remorse. General George Patton's memorable speech urging the killing of German captives during the invasion of Italy in 1943 vividly exemplifies this valorization of previously proscribed actions:

> When we meet the enemy, we will kill him. We will show him no mercy. He has killed thousands of your comrades, and he must die. If you company officers in leading your men against the enemy find him shooting at you and, when you get within two hundred yards of him, and he wishes to surrender, oh No! That bastard will die! You must kill him. Stick him between the third and fourth ribs. You will tell your men that. They must have the killer instinct. Tell them to stick him. He can do no good then. Stick them in the liver. We will get the names of

---

29 Nicholas Tavuchis, *Mea Culpa—A Sociology of Apology and Reconciliation*, Stanford U. Press, 1991, p. 7.

killers and killers are immortal. When word reaches him that he is being faced
with a killer battalion, a killer outfit, he will fight less.[30]

However brief this powerful speech, one can already identify in rough outline
the ideological reframing by which what was a moral taboo is transformed into
a moral imperative. Here we find the invoking of themes of retribution, self-
preservation, and dehumanization of the enemy that enable members to shift
between moral communities so that actions for which the community would
earlier have demanded extreme contrition are now viewed as essential for survival
and the protection of community.

But moral communities must be sustained in the present and not only by
moral exhortation. As Joanna Bourke makes clear in her enlightening history of
the emotional impact of "intimate killing" in World Wars I and II and during the
Vietnam War, unwanted expressions of remorse over killings were feared because
they could undermine morale as well as inhibit the aggression that was expected
from soldiers. Hence the pathologization of such feelings by psychiatrists
as abnormal, unmanly or "feminine" or neurasthenic implying a tendency to
use illness as a manipulative ploy or as a sign of weakness or psychological
ineffectuality and other designations suggesting this time a correlation between
the expression of remorse and a lack of character.[31] Lt. William Calley's response
to the charges brought against him testifies to the success of these prohibitions
against feelings of remorse. In March, 1971, after a lengthy and highly publicized
trial, Calley was convicted by a United States Military Court of the premeditated
murder of 22 infants, children, women, and old men in what came to be known as
the My Lai massacre during the war with Vietnam. The convictions represented
only a small proportion of the hundreds of killings for which Calley was originally
charged with murder. The court imposed a sentence of life imprisonment. Calley's
own response when he was first accused was one of disbelief and bewilderment:

> I couldn't understand it. I kept thinking though. I thought. Could it be I did
> something wrong? I knew that war's wrong. Killing's wrong: I realized that. I
> had gone to a war, though. I had killed, but I knew so did a million others. I sat
> there and I couldn't find the key. I pictured the people of My Lai: the bodies
> and they didn't bother me. I had found, I had closed with, I had destroyed the
> VC: the mission that day, I thought, it couldn't be wrong or I'd have remorse
> about it.[32]

30　James J. Weingartner, "Massacre at Biscari: Patton and an American War Crime,"
The Historian, Vol. l (ii), no. 2, 1989, p. 30.

31　Joanna Bourke, *An Intimate History of Killing: Face to Face Killing in 20th
Century Warfare*, Granta Books, 1999, pp. 242–249 *et passim*.

32　Bourke (1999), p. 159

But just in case such feelings should persist after discharge from the army as was observed among some of the veterans of Vietnam, another category could be applied- that of survivor's guilt—to suggest once again that the remorse that they felt was inappropriate, excessive, and unwarranted by their actions.[33] Indeed, it would take a collective assertion of will by veterans after the war to insist that they had the right to feel and to express remorse in a ceremony in which they cast off the medals they had been awarded for actions they now had come to abhor.[34] Thirty-eight years later, when Calley made a public statement that "there is not a day that goes by that I do not feel remorse for what happened that day in My Lai," it would be before an audience that by now had come to expect it.[35]

Other moments of visible and explicit intervention into the moral foundation of society are discernible as well in the efforts of new regimes as they seek to break with past practices. The attempt by the Nazis to transform the moral sentiments of German citizens towards mentally and physically disabled persons provides another striking illustration of how loyalty to community comes to be measured as much by a lack of remorse as by its obverse. Beginning in 1933, school children would be taken to asylums for the mentally ill, those who were neurologically impaired, and those who were severely physically disabled, there to gaze at the display of human misery because in the words of one instructor—"Every young person, every ethnic comrade of either sex who is interested in marrying must be led at least once through the screaming and nameless misery of an insane asylum, an institution for idiots, a residence for the crippled ... Here he shall learn to appreciate the sacred genetic inheritance he has received."[36] The purpose of these visits was to shift public perception from viewing the patients as sick persons who should be cared for by the community towards seeing them instead as objects of revulsion who were draining resources away from those who were healthy and could contribute to the new Germany. Here remorse over the mistreatment or neglect of the sick would be replaced by disgust over their physical imperfections and resentment at the burden that they placed on others.

However, we need not dwell on the extremes of war and revolutionary change to observe the collective work involved in the reshaping and monitoring of the moral emotions. Learning when remorse is appropriate and when it is not is a feature of all moral communities. Even if these expectations are unwritten, inchoate, and unenforced by any statute or diagnostic manual, this does not mean that their communication through approval and disapproval, acceptance and rejection, inclusion and avoidance are any the less effective as mediums of social regulation. Jennifer Hunt's ethnographic account of female cadets joining an urban

---

33   Bourke (1999), p. 238.

34   Shatan, Chaim F., "The Grief of Soldiers. Vietnam Combat Veterans' Self-Help Movement," *The American Journal of Orthopsychiatry,* 43, 4 (July, 1973).

35   Editorial, *New York Times,* August 28, 2009, p. A22.

36   Quoted from Claudia Koonz, *The Nazi Conscience,* Harvard University Press, 2003, p. 154.

police force in the northern United States captures well both the informality of the process by which neophytes learn of these expectations and their transformative impact nonetheless. In one riveting encounter, a female rookie responded to a complaint by a pedestrian that "something funny was going in the drugstore."[37] As Hunt describes the encounter, "the officer walked into the pharmacy where she found an armed man committing a robbery." When he pointed his gun at her, she "still pulled out her gun and pointed it at him." He ordered her to drop her gun telling her that "his partner was behind her with a revolver at her head." Again, she refused to lower her gun and the armed man and the rookie remained in a stalemate until another officer entered the premises and "ordered the suspect to drop his gun." Initially, she believed that she had acted appropriately in the situation in which she had stood up to the assailant and the confrontation had ended with no loss of life. The officers in the precinct however believed she had acted in a cowardly manner by not firing her weapon. Hunt reports that a few months later, the rookie "vehemently expressed the wish that she had killed the suspect and vowed that next time she would 'shoot first and ask questions later.'"[38] Other equally powerful vignettes convey the process by which the female cadet learns to overcome her initial reluctance to use lethal force and to view as normal and even courageous responses that earlier would have been accompanied by expressions of remorse.

It is through such processes that the expectations for membership in a moral community are communicated whether or not it is the suppression or expression of the moral emotions that becomes the standard by which loyalty to the community is demonstrated. Occasions for the demonstration of this loyalty arise when actions that are valorized or merely normalized in one group are condemned by another. It is these moments that both define and reinforce the boundaries within and between groups for it is here that the refusal to show remorse becomes simultaneously an affirmation of membership in one moral community and a measure of estrangement from the other. For a member to show remorse for actions that the community has deemed honorable or principled or courageous is tantamount to betrayal just as the refusal to show remorse for actions that are viewed as heinous are occasions for collective moral outrage.

If it is appreciated that demonstrations of remorse or its absence refer not just to the relationship between the individual and the victim but also to the relationship between the individual and the moral community, we can begin to understand why such moments can become the object of intense public scrutiny as well as occasions for the outpouring of passionate public responses. At stake in the decision of a court or a parole board or a tribunal to expect remorse or not

---

37 Jennifer Hunt, "Police Accounts of Normal Force," *Journal of Contemporary Ethnography,* 1985, Vol. 13, p. 321.

38 Hunt (1985), p. 322. For further elaboration on the requirements for membership in this moral community, see Jennifer Hunt and Peter Manning, "The Social Context of Police Lying," *Symbolic Interaction,* (1991) Vol. 14, no. 1, pp. 51–70.

to expect remorse is the choice between rival moral communities. Which moral community will be affirmed in such a contest—the community that condemns the act or the community that applauds the act?

To which moral community will the wrongdoer demonstrate their inmost loyalty and commitment and which will they betray through their expressions of remorse or refusals to show remorse? In Chapters 4 and 5, I analyze such moments of contestation in order to show how the remorse or absence of remorse of a wrongdoer can become a site of conflict between rival moral communities and between the state and the citizenry.

Remorse and the Construction of Moral Communities

But the expectation and expression of remorse play an even more pivotal role in the formation of moral communities than that of deciding the terms if and by which membership can be reestablished. The very process of deciding whether an action should call forth a show of remorse and how much remorse should be demonstrated is itself constitutive of the moral universe to which members of a moral community offer their allegiance. Analogous to Tavuchis's concept of "apologetic thresholds,"[39] these decisions establish the thresholds or limits that distinguish among those acts for which no remorse is expected, those acts for which a show of remorse is expected, and those acts that are perceived as so heinous that no quantum of remorse can restore the wrongdoer to membership in the moral community.

But these thresholds do not merely distinguish among acts—they also distinguish among persons. Expectations regarding remorse comprise what William Gamson has called the universe of obligations- that is, they constitute the "we" to whom specific obligations apply rather than the "them" to whom they do not apply.[40] They determine which groups or individuals are included within this universe-those persons whose suffering matters and to whom remorse is owed—and those persons whose suffering does not matter and to whom we do not owe remorse as we saw in the examples above regarding military conflict, revolutionary change, and the more mundane process of secondary socialization into a police force.

We can observe these processes in microcosm by looking at how characterizations of a wrongdoer as remorseful or unremorseful are used to support or challenge a request for the death penalty in a capital jury trial in the US. In the following example, the defendant, Steven Hayes, had been convicted of the murder of three members of a family in 2007 and the prosecution and defense have presented the jury with conflicting portrayals. According to the prosecution, the defendant is a "a con man so skillful at manipulation that the remorse he expressed could not be trusted." His performance is "an elaborate show to avoid a death

---

39   Tavuchis, p. 21.

40   William Gamson, "Hiroshima, The Holocaust, and the Politics of Exclusion," *American Sociological Review* 60 (1995) pp. 1–20.

sentence." According to the defense, however, he is described as "a shattered man," as engaged "in a perpetual struggle to understand his acts," and as someone who "would suffer through decades of remorse if sentenced to life in prison."[41]

Here we can see how both prosecution and defense have transformed the issue of whether or not Hayes deserves to die into a consideration of the quality and depth of his remorse. There is tacit agreement on both sides that the crime for which Hayes was convicted is sufficiently grave that it requires a demonstration of extreme suffering on the part of the wrongdoer and that this suffering must be for what he has done to the victim and not for the suffering inflicted on him as a result of his actions. In arguing in support of life over death, the defense has advanced the claim that Hayes will suffer for what he has done and that this suffering will be unending. It is then by virtue of this suffering that the argument for life over death can be supported. Because he will suffer as he should suffer, his suffering matters—arguably, from the vantage point of the defense, he is now one of the "we" towards whom we have obligations whether expressed in the form of mercy, forgiveness, or in this case, life without parole in place of death.

The prosecution has also seized upon the quality of Hayes's remorse as the measure of whether he deserves to live or die. But they have arrived at precisely the opposite conclusion to that of the defense. According to the prosecution, Hayes has no feelings of remorse for what he has done and hence he has not suffered and will not suffer for the harm that he has done. On this basis, arguably, from the vantage point of the prosecution, because he does not feel about what he has done the way he should feel, he has become one of the "them" towards whom the community may relinquish its obligations—someone towards whom the community need not show mercy or forgiveness.

In the remainder of this book, it is these processes by which moral communities constitute and reconstitute themselves through the degree of remorse they require from their members that will be one of the primary focuses of my analysis. In the course of analyzing these processes, I also want to show the work[42] that expectations of remorse do in terms of how the community acts towards the wrongdoer— how the perceived fulfillment of these expectations carries with it moral obligations in terms of how the community treats the wrongdoer while the failure to fulfill these expectations results in the relinquishing of these obligations.[43]

---

41   All quotes taken from William Glaberson, "Two Portraits of Triple Killer, Offered to Jurors, are at Odds," *New York Times,* October 29, 2010, p. A24.

42   I use the word "work" advisedly. As Sarah Ahmed has argued persuasively, naming emotions as well as attributing emotions shape our orientations toward the social objects that are so designated. It is in this sense that attributions of remorsefulness and remorselessness work to mobilize social action for or against the person so characterized. See Sarah Ahmed, *The Cultural Politics of Emotion,* Routledge, 2004.

43   See also path-breaking work by Martha Grace Duncan, "'So Young and So Untender': Remorseless Children and the Expectations of the Law," *Columbia Law Review,* Vol. 102, no. 6 (October, 2002), pp. 1469–1526, for analysis of how attributions

Towards a Constructionist Approach to the Study of Remorse

It is the central premise of this book that the regulative work of society extends not just to how members act whether in conformity or contravention of agreed upon rules but also how they feel about their actions or more precisely, how they express their feelings about their actions. In elaborating upon this proposition, my work builds on that strand of research within the sociology of affect that approaches emotion not as a raw visceral bodily sensation but rather as an event mediated by symbols and interpretations. I offer this cognitivist thesis without in any way seeking to deny or minimize the depth and intensity of suffering that is frequently claimed by and for persons who express remorse. That such feelings are mediated by social expectations whether explicit or tacit does not make them less real or less meaningful in their impact on those who experience them- indeed, the strength and intensity of these feelings can be taken as evidence of the indissoluble link between individual and society. Allegiance with or estrangement from a moral community at the core of one's identity is no trivial matter either from the standpoint of those to whom such feelings are ascribed or the group that ascribes them.

It is because I begin with this assumption of an inextricable social component in the production of expressions of remorse that I regard this work as a contribution to that larger project of dereification that has emerged over the past 40 years from the hybrid and interdisciplinary fields of cultural studies, critical semiotics, and interpretive sociology.[44] Instead of starting with the premise that we all have the same understanding about how feelings of remorse are expressed, when they should be expressed, and how they should be expressed to be credible, I approach each of these propositions as matters to be explained. I refer to this approach as involving a strategy of dereification because instead of treating categories such as "remorseful" or "remorseless" as self-evident—as if they were the same for all times and all places—I want to show how these categories are produced by tracing them back to the social contexts in which they arose. I hope to demonstrate through this approach that beliefs about whether remorse is appropriate, how it should be expressed, and how to detect true from genuine expressions of remorse differ for different groups and also differ for the same groups at different times.

The remaining chapters develop these ideas further. In Chapter 2, "Being and Doing: The Judicial Use of Remorse to Construct Character and Community,"

---

of remorselessness are deployed to override mitigation on the basis of "tender" age of the defendant.

44   The towering intellectual figure in this development is of course Michel Foucault whose recently translated lectures from the College de France are as good a place to start as any; see, for example, *Abnormal: Lectures at the College de France, 1973–1974,* Picador, 2003. But, as will become apparent, I draw my inspiration as well from an earlier generation of sociologists such as Goffman, Harold Garfinkel, and David Matza who initiated a similar intellectual sea change in the United States in the 1960s when they began to question the fixity of social categories.

I have drawn from a substantial body of case law generated from courts and tribunals in Canada between 2002 and 2004 to exemplify the social practices involved in the attribution of remorse. Here my concern is twofold. I have selected those judgments in which the credibility of remorse was a primary point of contention in order to elicit the most fully articulated statements of what courts look for in deciding whether a particular expression is genuine or not. But, equally importantly, my purpose is to unsettle the belief that remorse is a fixed category by showing the process of attribution at its moment of greatest elaboration and contentiousness. While I have used these texts to generate a profile of the feeling rules for the demonstration of remorse—those criteria that judges and tribunes use to recognize "real" remorse and to distinguish these expressions from less convincing demonstrations—I have also tried to show just how contingent and tenuous these attributions are. This tenuousness I argue is reflected not only in the disagreements between courts over what constitutes "real" remorse but the presence of compelling narratives and counter narratives that support or challenge each of the individual claims to have experienced "true" remorse.

In Chapter 3—"Making Monsters: Contemporary Uses of the Pathological Approach to Remorse"—I trace historically what I refer to as the pathological approach to the absence of remorse in which the transgressor who is perceived as unable to experience remorse is naturalized as different from the rest of humanity by virtue of psychological or biological deficiencies. I then show how this approach is deployed by prosecutors in a population of recent capital cases in the U.S. to help persuade jurors to decide in favor of the death penalty. In this analysis, my objective is to make visible the signifying power of attributions of remorse- how classification as remorseful or unremorseful is used to include or exclude wrongdoers from the category of those towards whom we have moral obligations.

In Chapter 4 entitled "Defiance," I look at the larger political dimensions of the regulation of expressions of remorse. No occasion in which remorse is expected reveals more fully what is at stake in these performances than when the person who has been judged guilty does not merely fail to demonstrate that their feelings of remorse are credible but proclaims and justifies their lack of remorse. It is at such moments that the passions that lie at the foundation of community surface into open view as the moral basis for the actions of the court is publicly challenged. In this chapter, I consider two such occasions—the first in which the wrongdoer acknowledges that they have committed the act for which they have been found guilty but counters the demand for remorse with a claim that the act was morally justifiable even if legally wrong. In the second site of contestation, I want to consider those who may well agree that what is legally wrong is also morally wrong but argue instead that the wrong person has been found guilty— and that they are innocent of the wrongs that been attributed to them.

In Chapter 5—"Remorse and Social Transformation"—I use transcripts, video footage, and first person accounts from the Truth and Reconciliation Commission Hearings held in South Africa from 1996–2000 to show that the transition in this society brought about by changes in governance and ideology also involved a reshaping of expectations for when expressions of remorse were appropriate and when they were not. Here I make use of concepts developed earlier in the book to show how through approval and disapproval, compliance with or resistance to the expectation of remorse, members negotiated the moral architecture of a newly emergent moral community. I argue that these processes in which courts and communities determine what actions require an expression of remorse and which actions do not—while more visible in moments of rapid political and ideological transition—are part of the effortful construction of shared sentiments even in societies undergoing less marked discontinuity.

Finally, in Chapter 6 entitled "The Social and Legal Regulation of Remorse," I identify the major themes of the foregoing analysis.

Chapter 2

Being and Doing:
The Judicial Use of Remorse to Construct
Character and Community[1]

In the summer and fall of 2009, two youths were brought to trial for a crime that captured the attention of the Canadian public as much for the comparatively tender age of the perpetrators as for its graphic violence. Both were charged and convicted of the murder of a 14-year-old girl. One of the accused, M.T.—a 15-year-old girl—pleaded not guilty. She would eventually be portrayed as the mastermind of the crime for having threatened to withhold sex and terminate her relationship with her boyfriend unless he killed the victim. The other accused, D.B.—her boyfriend aged 17 at the time—had stabbed the victim and left her bloodied and dying on a Toronto street on January 1, 2008. Unlike his co-accused, he would plead guilty to a charge of first-degree murder. The youth of the defendants, the complete absence of any provocation by the victim, and the gender reversal in which the younger female was cast as the "puppet master" and the older male "the puppet,"[2] helped to sustain public interest in the crime and the defendants.

But no event in the judicial and public recounting of the crime loomed larger than an interview with M.T. that was conducted by the police a day after the crime with M.T.'s mother allowed to be present. The interview was videotaped and some 18 months later, would be shown in court and disseminated to the public via the Internet. According to those who had watched it, what it revealed was M.T.'s "matter of fact answers" about her hatred of (the victim) and an absence of empathy and remorse that was so striking that "even her mother appeared taken aback."[3] This "obvious" lack of remorse would be referred to by the court in its pronouncement of sentence[4] and would become one of the grounds for which she was denied bail at the time of her arrest as well as one of the primary justifications

---

1 This chapter is an updated and revised version of an earlier article—Richard Weisman, "Being and Doing: The Judicial Use of Remorse to Construct Character and Community," *Social and Legal Studies,* Vol. 18, no. 1, 2009, pp. 47–69.

2 *R. v. Todorovic* [2009] Superior Ct. of Ontario, O.J., No. 3246 [33].

3 Shannon Kari, "Jury not told teen allegedly wanted nine dead: Defendant pushed boyfriend to kill: Crown," *National Post,* March 19, 2009, p. A6.

4 *R. v. Todorovic* [2009] [55].

for imposing an adult life sentence for murder rather than the more customary shorter parole period given to Canadian youths convicted of murder.[5]

Despite efforts by one of the psychiatrists who examined her to explain her appearance of "callousness, lack of empathy, and lack of remorse" as a difficulty in expressing emotion, the judge remarked that, "while I can appreciate that a person can be reticent to show emotion in public that they might exhibit in private, such reticence has to be evaluated against the nature of the event and the person's connection to it."[6] Two years later, after serving the first part of her sentence in a youth center, it would be on similar grounds that her application to delay her transfer to an adult facility would be denied. In the words of the Crown Prosecutor, she was someone whose remorselessness and striking "lack of empathy" demonstrated a "frightening character flaw."[7] He concluded that regardless of how well she met institutional expectations—she had been described by a case worker as a model inmate—until she developed insight into her crime or became involved in treatment, "she (would be) the person she was then (at the time of the murder)."[8]

D.B., on the other hand, would be cast in a different light. Apart from pleading guilty, he had read a statement at his sentencing hearing, which began as follows: "I stand here before you being sentenced for the disgusting crime I committed. Nothing I can say or do can right this wrong. I can't bring Stefanie back ... The only thing I can do is accept responsibility for my actions and express my deep sorrow and regret."[9] Moreover, according to the same report, he had demonstrated these feelings through his demeanor—with "his face reddening with what looked for all the world like shame" and his "head hung so low that from the side, it appeared he had none, that he had been beheaded."[10] These expressions would be acknowledged in the judgment when the court credited D.B. with remorse and compared him favorably to M.T.: "Unlike his former girlfriend, David seems capable of empathy and remorse. Indeed in his statement, David expressed in some detail his shame and regret and I believe he was entirely sincere when he did so."[11] The court predicted that, "if this trend continues ... if his progress continues, then the collective effect of those steps should provide a solid basis for (his) earlier return to society."[12]

---

5   More precisely, both parties were given adult life sentences in that for the rest of their lives, their liberty would be subject to conditions set by the National Parole Board. However, unlike adults convicted of first-degree murder, they could apply for parole after seven years rather than the 25-year minimum set for adults.

6   *R. v. Todorovic* [55].

7   Canadian Press, "Melissa Todorovic, Teen Murderer, Moving to Adult Jail," December 22, 2011, *Huffington Post Canada.*

8   ibid.

9   Christy Blatchford, " I have myself to blame for the decision I made that night," *Globe and Mail*, Sept. 18, 2009, p. A12.

10   ibid.

11   *R. v. Bagshaw* [2009] Superior Ct. of Ontario, O.J. 4123 [55].

12   *R. v. Bagshaw,* , O.J. 4123 [55].

I have chosen this case as an illustration of the points made in Chapter 1 and as a point of departure for the analysis to come. Here we can see how the attribution of remorse serves to attach or detach the perpetrator from the deed and to qualify or disqualify the doer as a member of the moral community. Because M.T. is perceived as without remorse in her first interview, and because she continues to be viewed as unremorseful when she applied to be allowed to stay at the youth center, she is "the person she was then"— her doing (her act of murder) continues to define her being (she is a murderer.) And because she does not feel remorse, she has "a frightening character flaw"—she is fundamentally different from those who belong to the moral community as voiced by the court and the reporters who covered the case. D.B., on the other hand, is seen through his words and demeanor to have demonstrated at least by the time of the sentencing that he is no longer the same person who committed the murder—he has professed remorse and he has shown on this body the shame and self-condemnation we would expect someone to feel as a member of the moral community. As a result, these different levels of remorse create a moral hierarchy in which his "earlier return to society" can be openly contemplated in a way that cannot be entertained for his former girlfriend.

In the following sections, I want to look more closely at this process by which the court ascribes remorse or its absence to the offender and distinguishes between those moral performances it finds credible and those it does not. It is a central premise of this work that these public occasions, in which there is both communal interest and communal reaction to a purported wrongdoer's remorse or absence of remorse, are significant events in the moral regulation of social life. The public and official focus on the inner life of the transgressor—whether it pertains to wrongs that have mobilized the outrage of the community or less sensational transgressions—informs us not just about the wrong itself but also about how someone who committed these wrongs should feel about their actions. It is these two features of the public display of remorse—both the communication of an expectation that remorse should be displayed, and then the evaluation of that display—that form the subject of the following analysis. What I hope to accomplish below is to show how the emotion of remorse is constituted in one of the primary sites for these public occasions—courts and tribunals—and how through the characterization of persons as remorseful or unremorseful, the larger community is instructed about when feelings of remorse are expected and when they are not as well as what form these feelings should take.

More particularly, my analysis is based on a close textual reading of a population of 178 Canadian cases decided between 2002–2004 in which the remorse of the offender or wrongdoer was a matter of dispute between those who spoke for or against his or her claims to remorse. I generated this population by using the *LexisNexis* legal database to search for all cases during this two-year period in which remorse or its truncations were mentioned at least five times.[13] I drew this

---

13 I used the search term "atleast5(remors!)" to generate my populations of cases and conducted the search on July 1, 2007. The population includes all judgments that met this

population from all areas of Canadian law in which designations of transgressors as remorseful or not are deployed as grounds for inclusion or expulsion from their occupation, their country of choice, from civil society, or from any other community of reference. The threshold of five was selected in order to identify those cases in which the category was most fully elaborated, either because it was contested or because it figured prominently in the judgment. I imposed this restriction since the goal of my inquiry was not merely to catalog the frequency with which the category was used but to elicit as fully as possible the criteria used in judicial discourse to characterize an offender as remorseful or without remorse. The present analysis is anchored in the assumption that because of their greater attempt at explication, these cases will be the most helpful in bringing out the role of the court as actively constituting what remorse means and how it is expected to be demonstrated. My discussion below is based on my identification of recurrent patterns in the types of evidence invoked by these judgments to confirm or disconfirm the presence of remorse.

Before undertaking this analysis, however, it is necessary to locate the place of remorse in the context of Canadian legal discourse.

Canadian Legal Discourse and the Remorseful Transgressor

In Canadian legal discourse, the division of offenders into those who show remorse and those who do not is by no means restricted to criminal law although the designation serves much the same purpose whether applied to labor grievances, disciplinary proceedings in law and medicine, hearings over eligibility for immigration, or other areas of law. What these different sites have in common is the decision over whether to include or exclude the transgressor as a member of the community in relation to which the transgression occurred. In the context of labor law, considerations of remorse enter into decisions by arbitrators over whether persons who have been dismissed with cause from their employment will be reinstated with or without penalty; those whose remorse is deemed absent or insufficient—the determination of which is the subject of this analysis—are more likely to have their dismissal upheld. In disciplinary hearings before the relevant law societies or medical boards, attributions of remorse are also used analogously to distinguish among those transgressors who will be admitted or refused admission to the bar, or granted or refused permission to continue their practice whether in law and medicine. In the analysis below, all of these judicial glosses will be treated as part of the body of decision-making that tells us what remorse means in legal discourse.

But Canadian judicial discourse about remorse cannot be understood apart from one its most distinctive features—that is the non-recognition of remorse in precedent or statute and, consequently, the general absence of any restriction

---

condition between January 1, 2002 and June 30, 2004.

or guidance in its formulation.[14] While there exists an ever-increasing body of precedents regulating when remorse or its absence may be invoked as a factor in sentencing, how remorse is defined and how it is determined are entirely open-ended in its judicial rendering. What this means in practice is that there is no linguistic or conceptual gulf between popular and other extra-legal conceptions of remorse and how remorse is conceived in law—judicial talk about remorse simply replicates the popular or expert understandings from which it draws. This open-endedness applies equally to the evidence on which the attribution of remorse is founded—direct observation, expert testimony, pre-sentence reports, police reports, or observations by any others with whom the offender was in contact or any combination of the above can be marshaled in support of or in opposition to the claim that the offender was remorseful. If the evidentiary rules by which guilt and innocence are decided are governed by legal norms, it is social convention that governs the attribution of remorse or its absence.

Yet if legal discourse about remorse is rooted in popular understandings of the emotion, it is still a discourse in which concepts are elaborated far beyond their usage in everyday speech. In its most quotidian form, remorse is the credit given to those who admit to guilt and other delicts for which they have been charged. Simple, behavioral, and unexamined the category would remain if it did not play so crucial a role in the legal forum in crediting or discrediting character. But it is through remorse that the world is divided not just into those who transgress, but also into those whose misconduct will come to define their character and those whose character will lead us to redefine their misconduct. The result is an ever-expanding narrative of what makes a claim to remorse credible or not and what expressions of character are perceived by the court as separating the offender from the act or aligning the offender with the act. To do justice to this wealth of material, I have identified several analytically and empirically distinct usages of the concept in terms of how it is rendered in judicial or adjudicative speech. First, there is the equating of remorse with the admission of responsibility and here I seek to bring out the judicial expectations over what is sufficient to qualify as an admission and what is not. Second, there is the showing of remorse through gestural expressions or what Goffman has referred to as "body glosses"[15] in which the offender is judged as credible or not depending on the feelings that are displayed. Here I look at

---

14 Despite efforts by the US Sentencing Commission to standardize and simplify the process by which remorse is identified, in practice, the same open-endedness that characterizes Canadian judicial discourse practice is true of American judicial discourse as well. For discussion of how this gap between policy and practice evolved, see Michael O'Hear, "The Federal Sentencing Guidelines: Ten Years Later: Remorse, Cooperation and 'Acceptance of Responsibility': The Structure, Implementation, and Reform of Section 3E1.1 of the Federal Sentencing Guidelines," 91 *Northwestern University Law Review*, Summer, 1997, see pp. 1512 et passim.

15 Erving Goffman, *Relations in Public: Microstudies in Public Order*, New York: Basic Books, 1972, p. 11.

judicial expectations concerning what an offender should feel and should express if their display of remorse is to be accredited as real and spontaneous as opposed to contrived or strategic. Finally, I look at the third major indicia of remorse— whether, or in what way, the offender has undergone personal transformation. In this part of the analysis, I look at the vocabularies of change that are accepted by courts as evidence that the remorseful person is no longer the same person who committed the offending act. For purposes of clarity, I will treat each of these usages separately before I bring them together into a composite description of how the remorseful offender is constituted in judicial speech.

Constituting the Remorseful Transgressor in Canadian Law

Admission of Responsibility

On one level, the admission of responsibility for the offence or transgression would appear to be the most straightforward criterion for deciding whether the offender has demonstrated remorse—a plea of guilty, one might assume, would suffice to meet this expectation. Yet the more extended cases on the subject and the heightened scrutiny that they reflect reveal a far more complex understanding of what is entailed in admitting responsibility as well as a rich repertory from a judicial perspective of all that can go wrong in meeting this expectation. I quote at length from the following case involving the shoplifting of an item from a department store because it makes explicit what is unstated in most of the other decisions—namely, the expectation that the remorseful offender acknowledge their agency in perpetrating the offence:

> When I read the pre-sentence report, I note ... where the author of the report states: 'The offender has not taken responsibility for the offense before the court and indicated that this was not an intentional offence but a **situational offence**.' [my emphasis]
>
> Counsel for the defense has tried to somehow explain that sentence. But I find it has not really been explained in a way to engender a confidence that the accused has taken a moral responsibility of what this court has found he has done on the evidence before it.
>
> If there is no admittance, in my view, that is something over which the court has the jurisdiction to admit some leniency, then of course the Court will feel that there is nothing really remorseful ... (which the court) can consider (in mitigation.) Here we have no such situation. We have an individual who stands by his story, but now framed in such a way to say what he did was situational. ...
>
> By the evidence before this Court, a determination has been made. And this court found that it was a deliberate act. He may not wish to admit it. He may wish to still, as the Crown says, consider his reputation, that he's not a thief. As

I said, only one who admits that they have done a wrong can seek some mercy for the wrong which they have committed.[16]

For present purposes, two points are noteworthy in this excerpt. First, the offender has failed to show remorse because he has defined his criminal act as situational—that is, as an act that was outside his control rather than as an act over which he had control. In effect, to demonstrate remorse, he must characterize the transgressive act as one that he has chosen to do. Second, we encounter one of the central paradoxes in the attribution of remorse. In order to qualify for the mercy of the court, the offender must identify himself with his wrongful act—mitigation is conferred upon the remorseful only because it is gratuitous. To portray one's self as not responsible for one's transgressive behavior is to suggest that whatever punishment is meted out is undeserved. However, to come before the court and to fully acknowledge not only that one has committed the wrongful act but that it was a product of one's free will is to claim that the punishment is in fact deserved. By acknowledging the moral authority of the court to impose punishment, the remorseful offender has a claim to the court's mercy or, in this case, the benefit of mitigation. By questioning this moral authority, by claiming that the act in question was not one for which the offender was responsible, the unremorseful or less than remorseful sacrifice the benefit of mercy.[17]

Another case further illustrates the judicial insistence on the acknowledgment of agency in what might well be more challenging circumstances. Here, the offender was convicted of dangerous driving causing death and claimed as evidence of her remorse that she felt sorrow and grief over the death of the victim and that she had participated in various ceremonies in order to seek healing and peace for the family as part of her aboriginal religious beliefs. But when the psychologist who appeared for the defence was asked whether "she (the offender) had expressed … that she was responsible for the collision and the death of the (victim), the response was (that) "she accepts that she was part of a tragedy that took a young life." In pronouncing sentence, the judge stated that, "this, in my view, is not the same as remorse and acceptance of responsibility … there is in this case clearly no acceptance of responsibility which might have served as a mitigating factor."[18] When confronted with a defense that claimed that the offender understood remorse

---

16   *R. v. Callahan* [2003] N.S.C., Lexis 350, p. 9.

17   Thus serving a legitimating function similar to what Hay (1975) and Strange (1996) have suggested in their discussion of mercy. Remorse must be expressed in such a way as to justify the right of the state to use force against the accused. Only after the accused has upheld the rightfulness of this use of force may the law mercifully decide against using that right. Hence the usage preserves the official distinction between clemency and mercy (Kobil, 2007) with the former referring to punishment that is not deserved and the latter to punishment deserved but not imposed.

18   *R. v. Galloway* [2004] Sask. C.A., 187 C.C.C. (3rd), p. 369.

differently from the standpoint of her own culture, the court affirmed the non-negotiability of acknowledgment of agency as a condition for remorse.

But even among those who do admit agency for what they have done, there are additional expectations that must be met for a claim of remorse to be validated. It follows from the above that the remorseful offender is someone who offers no excuses or justifications for their misconduct. Those who "minimize or rationalize their conduct"[19] or "redirect responsibility away from themselves"[20] fail to show remorse. One offender who was convicted of manslaughter "rather than display(ing) recognition of his responsibility, blames his alcohol and drug addiction,"[21] while another offender also convicted of manslaughter is credited with remorse because, while "he admits to being intoxicated at the time of his encounter with (the victim), he) does not use it to excuse his behavior."[22] Justifications for misconduct such as the contention of an offender convicted of fraud that "other car businesses do the same thing"[23] similarly nullify characterization as a remorseful offender. As one arbitrator expressed it, remorse requires a "full acceptance of responsibility" with no invoking of excuses or "stressful circumstances" however much "that is certainly a natural response."[24]

It is perhaps not surprising that, in the population under review, the majority of offenders or grievers who appeared before their adjudicator failed to show remorse according to this first criterion. Probably the dominant mode of explanation in the social sciences for accounting for the reluctance of rule-breakers to accept full responsibility for their wrongdoing is still neutralization theory as articulated some 50 years ago in the classic work of Gresham Sykes and David Matza.[25] The primary thrust of this approach is to suggest that those who break the rules of their community but who remain attached to its values will seek to "neutralize" or diminish social condemnation as well as self-reproach by accounting for their actions in ways that reduce their culpability. Moreover, these accounts or "techniques" will pattern themselves after what are perceived as the existing repertory of socially acceptable excuses or justifications. Hence, the person who is convicted of sexual interference but claims that his victims were not damaged by his actions or the auto worker who attributes his physical altercation with a fellow worker to his long-term depression, or the griever who reproaches his employers and accusers as irresponsible and incompetent, or the offender who has been convicted of fraud for rolling back odometers and who claims that this is normal practice for

---

19   *Manitoba and M.G.E.U.* [2003], 121 L.A.C. (4th), 114.

20   *R. v. Pellizzon* [2003], A.J. Lexis 1433, p. 10.

21   *R. v. La Fantaisie* [2004], AB.C., Lexis 696, p. 4.

22   *R. v. P (B.W.)* [2003], W.C.B.J., Lexis 1720, p. 2.

23   *R. v. MacAdam* [2003], P.E.I.S.C., 171 C.C.C. (3rd) 481.

24   *Re Brewers Distribution Ltd and Distillery Worker's Union, Local 300* [2003] C.L.A.S.J., Lexis 1464, p. 48.

25   Gresham Sykes and David Matza, "Techniques of Neutralization: A Theory of Delinquency," *American Sociological Review* 22 (1957): pp. 664–670.

persons in his occupation exemplify one or more of the "techniques" identified by the authors in which the offender seeks to deflect blame away from themselves on to the victim or the situation. The truly remorseful person, on the other hand, as conceived by the court or tribunal, however, is someone who makes use of none of these devices for diminishing their responsibility for the misconduct for which they have been charged. What Sykes and Matza saw as the deployment of widely available, self-justifying rationales for social and legal transgressions and what Maruna and Copes have referred to as the "normality of neutralization"[26] has been pathologized in judicial discourse as "minimization", a term that is mentioned in seven of the cases included in this population and referred to in one case as having an impact "on the genuineness of remorse which in turn detract(s) from a positive attitude towards reformation and rehabilitation."[27] Far from trying to blunt social condemnation by invoking circumstance or contingency and far from seeking mitigation by redirecting blame to other causes, those who demonstrate remorse are expected to portray themselves as deserving of whatever social disapproval or punishment they may receive for their choice to commit an act they knew to be morally wrong.

Yet, the deeper importance of this criterion of accepting responsibility is the control it exercises over the crime narrative or the narrative of the wrongdoing. As stated in one judgment, "there are many reported cases involving guilty pleas which, by itself, is a sign of remorse where there have been findings that there was no remorse in a factual sense and where there was found to be a lack of insight into conduct in question."[28] In this instance, the offender is viewed as lacking in remorse despite her guilty plea because she disagrees with the factual conclusions reached by the court. A labor arbitration hearing in which the griever is challenging the termination of his employment even more fully illustrates the control that the attribution of remorse exerts over the content of the conflict. In this instance, the worker in question, a health care aide at a nursing home, had been fired in part for his breach of fidelity when, after the death of a resident, he had left a note that "could imply that the death was not accidental" and that it may have been the result of understaffing. According to the employer, the worker had shown "defiance and disdain (towards the employer) and hence was not remorseful for his conduct."[29] In this case, the arbitrator concluded that while the worker's "expressions of remorse" were "tenuous"—that is, he did not admit that his actions were wrongful, "the absence of a clear acknowledgment that the home was … not understaffed the day (the resident) died"[30] gave support to what the worker had claimed. In other instances, however, failure to fully concur with all the charges that have

---

26 Shadd Maruna and Heith Copes, "What Have We Learned from Five Decades of Neutralization Research?" *Crime and Justice* 32 (2005), pp. 221–320 at p. 285.

27 *R. v. Bilton* [2003], Ontario Ct. of Justice, Lexis 4338 [46].

28 *R. v. E.M.S.* [2003], Ontario Superior Ct. of Justice, Lexis 110 [8].

29 *Re Meadow Park and CAW Local* [2003], Lexis 1333, p. 437.

30 ibid p. 444.

been brought, or unwillingness to accept without qualification the official version of the crime or the wrongdoing can be taken as a lack of remorse. In another case in which the employee who was dismissed wrote a letter in which he stated "I would like to express my deepest remorse, regret and most sincere apology for my behavior towards the company and (co-worker whom he physically attacked),"[31] the claim to remorse is rejected because the worker did not mention all the unacceptable actions in which he was found to have engaged. Similarly, claiming provocation by another worker, when this has not been recognized by the court, also will disqualify a claim to remorse. Acceptance of responsibility as a criterion for the attribution of remorse entails a full agreement with exactly how the crime or the wrongdoing has been conceived by the court or tribunal.

But how do we know that this willingness to take responsibility and to throw one's self open to the mercy of the court reflects the offender's feelings about their own misconduct especially since these actions, if believed, will result in tangible benefits? It is here that the court looks to what I have referred to as the second component of remorse—the feelings that accompany this willingness to take responsibility for one's misconduct. How is remorse shown such that the court or tribunal can conclude that the wrongdoer's public expressions correspond to what is felt and can therefore be perceived as revealing his or her true character? I now turn to this component of judicial discourse about remorse.

Showing One's "True" Feelings

It is yet another paradox in the process by which transgressors are characterized that the most elusive and least articulated of all criteria should also be the most important. For it is the affect that accompanies the verbal claim—in effect, the paralinguistic cues—that is perceived as the true window to the person's essence. The words may speak of acceptance of responsibility or sincere contrition but it is through the feelings that are demonstrated whether to the adjudicator or to another credible authority that the court believes it can take the true measure of the person before them.

But even if there is no currently available means by which abstract emotions such as remorse, guilt, or shame can be reliably correlated with their empirical manifestations, it is clear that the reading and valuing of emotions is very much contingent on the discursive lens through which they are viewed. Moral philosophers posit significant distinctions among shame, guilt, and remorse in terms of how they contribute to ethical behavior—distinctions that are virtually ignored in legal discourse.[32] Similarly, the lively debate among social anthropologists, sociologists, and clinicians over whether shame or guilt is the more socially and morally useful

---

31 *Re Accuride and C.A.W. Canada, Local 27* [2004], C.L.A.S.J., Lexis 255 [9].

32 For a nuanced discussion of moral emotions that tries to distinguish between suffering that is empathic and suffering that is focused on the self, see Gabrielle Taylor, *Pride, Shame and Guilt: Emotions of Self-Assessment,* New York: Oxford University Press,

emotion to motivate adherence to ethical norms has had little impact on a discourse in which shame, guilt, and remorse are often conflated into one category.[33] And, as we shall below, even therapeutic discourse which has far greater input into the creation and application of legal categories than other disciplinary languages, would likely view as pathological the very expressions of remorse that from a juridical standpoint establish character. This is by no means to suggest that legal discourse is without nuance and fine distinctions of its own—that it is not in its own way as elaborated a language as the more academic disciplines from which it selectively draws. What is important to recognize is that the distinctions that are emphasized, as well as those that are ignored, arise from a particular discursive framework.

I use the following case to introduce the central dimensions by which remorse as emotion is identified as real or spurious in legal discourse. In this instance, a Committee from The Law Society of Upper Canada is deliberating over whether to admit to the bar a candidate who has up to this point satisfied all the academic and professional requirements for admission but whose final acceptance turns on the issue of whether he is of good character as required under a section of the Law Society Act.[34] The committee's inquiry is focused on his sexual misconduct with several children with whom he was in a position of trust. One of the children was an eight-year-old girl—described in the judgment as "profoundly deaf"—with whom he embarked on an active sexual relationship when she was nine that did not completely end until she was 16. The other was a sexual relationship with his own daughter that began when she was four and ended only when the mother of the child—who had earlier been a co-participant—brought a complaint to the police. By the time of the hearing, Mr. P. had already served his sentence, which consisted of a term of incarceration plus a three-year period of probation. Ultimately, in its decision, the committee acknowledged that his admission to the Law Society would turn on whether the members believed that his expressions of remorse were real: "The Committee must now decide whether the applicant's remorse is genuine or strategic and whether his inclinations to rationalize and justify his criminal behavior have been overcome."[35] At the same time, the judgment explicitly recognized the high stakes involved and that "for Mr. P., the motivation to express remorse is very great." In effect, the task of adjudication required that the committee decide whether Mr. P.'s expression of remorse reflected his inner

---

1985 and Steven Tudor, *Compassion and Remorse: Acknowledging the Suffering Other*, Leuven: Peeters, 2001.

33 Notable among significant contributions to this debate is Thomas Scheff's work on shame—see, especially, Scheff, 2000, "Shame and the Social Bond: A Sociological Theory," *Sociological Theory* 18 (2000), pp. 84–99.

34 *P. (D.M.) (Re)* O.J., 1989. I have relied on a case decided earlier than the other cases in my population because it offers the fullest elaboration of any of the judgments I have reviewed of how the feeling of remorse is expected to be communicated.

35 ibid [27].

belief that what he did was morally reprehensible or whether it was merely a ploy to obtain the benefit of admission. Here is their statement of how they decided it was the latter rather than the former:

> Mr. P's overall deportment throughout these proceedings is relevant to the Committee's assessment of his credibility. When pressed about whether or not he believed that his actions had caused harm to his young victims, he was defensive and evasive. He gave his evidence listlessly, in monotone, except when he spoke about his desire to practice law. Then he spoke with emotion, with conviction. By contrast, he seemed somewhat indifferent to whether or not he had done harm to the children.[36]

It was the absence of emotion to which the committee referred in its rejection of Mr. P.'s expression of remorse as inauthentic and devoid of credibility. But what is the expression that will make credible the transgressor's claim to feel remorse? What the juridical responses have in common is the expectation that someone who is truly remorseful will suffer for their transgression and that this suffering will be visible. Thus, in a case of criminal negligence causing the death of a seven-month-old child under her care, the offender is credited with "extreme remorse" for her misconduct by virtue of the emotional pain that she is perceived to be experiencing—"I do not doubt that she is haunted continuously by the memory of the injury she caused to (the victim)."[37] In another case, in which the offender was convicted of sexual abuse of his stepdaughters, the courts takes as evidence of his "genuine and profound sense of remorse, that he became depressed, so much so (that) he needed professional assistance."[38] Or in a case involving impaired driving causing death, the transgressor is characterized as "extremely remorseful and sincere in his expression of sadness" after he told the court that "he wish(ed) there was a word that was bigger and greater than the word sorry" and "that he had difficulty eating or sleeping, thinking about the loss that the family (of his victim) had suffered."[39] Other similar symptoms connoting extreme suffering and taken as indicators of "extreme" remorse include "feelings of sickness," "overwhelming guilt," "crying," and expressions of "shame." In the absence of direct demonstrations of visible suffering or psychiatric reports that are taken as valid characterizations of the offender's state of remorsefulness, reports by other officials such as investigating officers or probation officers of the offender's "visible distress" or that they were "very upset" or "extremely emotional" are also sometimes offered in support of establishing the credibility of the claim.

But if extreme distress establishes the character of the offender as remorseful, it is equally clear that the lack of distress when it is expected demonstrates the

---

36   ibid.

37   *R. v. Lam* [2004], Alberta Ct. of Queen's Bench. Lexis 112, [20].

38   *R. v. M.S.* [2003], Sask. Ct. of Appeal, Lexis 94, [30].

39   *R. v. Kaserbauer* [2003], Manitoba Ct. of Queen's Bench, Lexis 204 [4].

absence of remorse. Hence, the court could observe, in a case involving a youth charged with a gang-related murder, that he demonstrated no remorse because he "was not devastated by the situation in which he found himself" nor "horrified" enough not to associate with his fellow gang members.[40] In another instance, the offender who was convicted of aggravated assault is described as "remarkable for (the) casualness (of his conversation) and lack of real remorse."[41] He is further characterized as someone who "is perhaps incapable of arriving at a level of remorse necessary to relate to what he has done on a high emotional level." Still others are characterized as not remorseful even if they have pleaded guilty if they discuss their offenses without "appropriate affect": "half-heartedness", "slouch(ing) in one's chair", (being) "cold and dispassionate," and "verbalization ... with an air of superficiality," are other terms used to describe someone whose moral performance is perceived as inconsistent with their claim to remorse.[42] The remorseful offender is expected to show on their body and in their demeanor that they have suffered or are suffering for their wrongdoing.

If the terms in which the remorseful offender accepts responsibility deprive him or her of any claim to mitigation other than that of mercy, the sense of unworthiness that is communicated through words must be matched by gestures that demonstrate that these words correspond to what is felt. In place of the denunciation of the court is the demonstrable self-condemnation of the transgressor. It is the exposure of these feelings to public view that enables the court to verify that the offender's "true" self has been affected by their misconduct. In this self-identification of act with being, as well as in the spontaneous gestures of what are taken as signs of low self-regard, the offender reveals the extent of their suffering for having transgressed the norms of community. Indeed, it is the absence of suffering—the ability to maintain a calm demeanor, to avoid flooding out—that is likely to draw the court's outrage, as exemplified by such phrases as, "he showed not a scintilla of remorse."[43]

But it is important that one be precise about the type of suffering that the court expects from the offender. For his or her claim to be validated, the wrongdoer must suffer for the suffering that he caused rather than for the suffering he has endured. As one judge stated in assessing the remorsefulness of an offender who was convicted of dangerous driving causing death: "It is not clear, though, that one can distinguish the possibility of some remorse from the constellation of

---

40   *R. v. (C.V.)* [2002], Ontario Ct. of Justice, Lexis 69 [47].

41   *R. v. Cooper* [2002], Newfoundland and Labrador Supreme Ct., Lexis 456 [32].

42   These phrases are taken from the following cases respectively: *Orca Bay Sports and Entertainment and Hotel, Restaurant, and Culinary Employees and Bartender Union* [2002], B.C.P.L.A.J., 902; *Quality Meat Packer Ltd. and U.F.C. W. Local 175/633*, Ontario [2002], C.L.A.S.J.; *R. v. Ervin* [2003] Alberta Ct. of Appeal, [2003]; *R. v. J.F.H.* [2002], Ontario Superior Ct. of Justice, Lexis 822 [6].

43   *R. v. D.B.B.* [2004], Ontario Superior Ct. of Justice , Lexis 1404.

difficulties that the defendant faced throughout that time after the incident."[44] Or, in another instance, in which the accused was convicted of molesting two of his stepsons, the pre-sentence report is cited in the judgment as acknowledging his distress but questions whether "he is more focused on the effect the offences have had on his own life."[45] The suffering of the remorseful offender is expected to be empathic and oriented to the other rather than to the offender's own emotional pain. From this vantage point, even the most drastic of responses to one's offense such as attempted suicide can be doubted as an expression of remorse if, as one judge surmised, it "could equally be interpreted as a means of escape from responsibility."[46] Suffering that is suspected to be self-serving or self-oriented is antithetical to the judicial perception of how true remorse should be demonstrated. In its shaping of how remorse should be demonstrated by approving those expressions of affect that are taken as real and rejecting those expressions that are perceived as superficial, strategic, or insufficient, judicial discourse both affirms and constitutes what, following Hochschild, I have called the "feeling rules" of the community, both how a member of the moral community should feel about their misconduct and how these feelings should be expressed.

The splitting of self, mentioned by Goffman in relation to apology, takes a particular form in juridical discourse in relation to remorse. If the remorseful offender is obliged to avow their unqualified responsibility for their misconduct, it is through their emotional display that they demonstrate the separation between themselves and their act. It is here that the remorseful offender does not merely adopt the standpoint of the community towards their wrongdoing—he or she demonstrates through their visible suffering and self-infliction of punishment their rejection of that part of the self that committed the wrongdoing. Hence, the offender's "hauntedness," self-loathing, or depressive demeanor can be valorized in law as moral condemnation of the self that betrayed community even if pathologized in psychology as symptoms of mental disorder.

The avowal of responsibility for the act coupled with the offender's demonstration of self-condemnation enacts the tension between doing and being—the offender has chosen to act in a manner that betrays community but they have shown on their body that they are loyal to community. It is in the third usage of remorse that the separation between act and being is concretized as the offender sheds the self that perpetrated the transgressive act by embarking on a project of self-transformation.

Remorse and Self-Transformation

It is the third criterion for validating a claim of remorse that is potentially the most expansive of all because it widens the involvement of the state in managing

---

44   *R. v. Gratton* [2003], Alberta Ct. of Queen's Bench, Lexis 109 [7].

45   *R. v. T.E.* [2003], British Columbia Provincial Ct., Lexis 4587 [23].

46   *R. v. Cairns* [2004], BC Ct. of Appeal, Lexis 829, p. 30.

the offender. From this vantage point, the proof of remorse consists not just in the acknowledgment of responsibility and the demonstration of visible suffering for one's wrongdoing, but in the willingness of the offender to make fundamental changes in one's character so that the wrongdoing will not recur. Here, the task of the remorseful offender or their advocates is to show to the satisfaction of the court that they are no longer the person who perpetrated the transgression—that they are taking or have taken steps to renounce those parts of the self that led to the misconduct and to develop a new self for whom such actions would no longer be possible. The transgressive act becomes the occasion for the wrongdoer to affect a radical rupture with the past; in turn, remorse is demonstrated by abandoning previously cherished ways of seeing, by changing one's lifestyle, or by other means of effecting deep characterological transformations. What is offered as evidence of remorse is engagement with those identity-transforming institutions that are believed by the court to bring about these profound inner changes.[47]

Thus, in one case in which the offender had been convicted of kidnapping and assault causing bodily harm, the judged observed of the offender that, "the remorse he expresses may have some substance. I have heard as well not only the words of (the offender) in his comments to the court about his acceptance of responsibility and his intention to continue his progress ... I have also had the opportunity of assessing his commitment to change subjectively."[48] Similarly, there is a promise of significant change in another case in which a father who was convicted of assaulting his daughter for hitting her in the face after she refused to admit she had stolen something, spoke to the court as evidence of his remorsefulness- " ... I have completed both courses that were mentioned earlier (there), the anger management and parenting course, and I have a lot of comments about it from friends noticing a big change with myself, nothing more important than my children, they have noticed a drastic difference within myself. I have learned new ways to control the emotion of anger."[49] Or, in another instance in which the offender had pleaded guilty to several counts of robbery, defense counsel submitted as evidence of the depth of his remorse and by virtue of his participation in a halfway house, letters of reference from staff in that program, that his client is a "different person today from the individual involved in the criminal activities described."[50] More typical are statements that the offender has undertaken therapy or entered a program

---

47   See Lonnie Athens, "Dramatic Self-Change," *Sociological Quarterly* 36:3 (1995), pp. 581–586 for what is still one of the better discussions of the social processes involved in identity transformation; for some of the more well-known narratives of personal transformation among persons who were convicted of capital crimes in the US, see Beverly Lowry, *Crossed Over: A Murder, A Memoir,* Vintage Books, 1992 and Louis Nizer, *The Jury Returns,* Doubleday, Garden City, New York, 1966, for accounts of Karla Fae Tucker and Paul Crump, respectively.

48   *R. v. McBride* [2003], Nova Scotia Supreme Ct., Lexis 2334, p. 38.

49   *R. v. D.A.* [2004], New Brunswick Ct. of Queen's Bench [6].

50   *R. v. Clarke* [2002], BC Provincial Court, Lexis 4304 [18].

such as Alcoholics Anonymous or promised to strive for "an exemplary lifestyle" all taken by the court as evidence of "sincere remorse" or "consistent with the statement that the (offender) is remorseful about these events."

If we combine the aforementioned three criteria, we can begin to identify the main contours of the moral performance that is entailed in the showing of remorse before the court or tribunal. The remorseful wrongdoer is someone who acknowledges, without excuse or justification his or her responsibility for the wrongdoing. Moreover, the wrongdoer accepts without modification how judicial authority has constituted the act of misconduct. The test of whether this claim reveals the true character of the wrongdoer consists in the demonstration of how he or she feels about what they have done. The wrongdoer is expected to demonstrate that they have suffered for their wrongdoing. But the suffering is expected to take the form of shame over one's actions—that is, a lowering of self-regard or self-esteem as a result of perpetrating the wrongful act—rather than disclosure of one's own victimization as a result of any punishments that are imposed. The wrongdoer suffers visibly but does not portray him or herself as a victim. Finally, the wrongdoer promises to undergo, or has already undergone, a process of self-transformation in which those parts of the former self that contributed to the misconduct or betrayed the moral community, are replaced by a new self that is committed to the moral community. It is this typology of acknowledgment of wrongdoing, suffering for one's wrongdoing, and personal epiphany that will be illustrated in the two legal vignettes to be discussed in the next section.

Remorse and the Crime Narrative—Two Illustrations

I use the following two cases to show how the crime narrative of the remorseful offender incorporates the aforementioned typology of acknowledgment, suffering, and transformation. I chose these cases for three reasons—each focuses on the offender's remorsefulness as a central consideration in arriving at an appropriate sentence, each designates the offender as remorseful and gives reasons for their conclusion, and each in everyday language credits the offender as someone who is not defined by their wrongdoing.

The first case involves a man, Mr. R., who served as parish priest in a rural outpost.[51] Approximately 20 years before his trial, he became sexually involved with one of his altar boys, aged about 13 at the time. What had begun with intimate conversations about the boy's problems at home led to discussions "about puberty and his own sexual desires."[52] These discussions were followed by advances, which eventually developed into a furtive relationship that lasted for three years. One day, when the boy was 16, his mother found a letter that her son had written to Mr. R. that she "described ... as pornographic filth."[53] The father then contacted

---

51   *R. v. Cromien* [2001] (T.) Ontario Superior Ct. of Justice, Lexis 2173.
52   ibid [4].
53   ibid [6].

the supervisor of Mr. R.'s religious order, wrote Mr. R. a letter, and received a letter of apology in return. The matter was investigated by the local police at that time but no charges were laid until 20 years later, by which time the victim was in his mid-thirties.

In the intervening years, Mr. R. had left the priesthood even though he was given the option to remain. He left because, in his own words, he "had betrayed (the victim) as a Priest."[54] Subsequent to his departure from the priesthood, he had married and become a father with one child. Mr. R.'s request for leave from the religious community, his later involvement in counseling, and his application for dispensation of his priestly vows were all presented by the court as evidence of "deep remorse." In an allocution to the court, Mr. R. stated that:

> I realized when I got a letter from (the father of the boy) that I had been really acting wrongly and I immediately sent a letter of apology to the whole family expressing my sorrow... I was really shattered by that letter and shattered also, at the fact that not only had I betrayed M. (the victim) and his family, but everybody and I decided I would leave the priesthood as my part of the responsibility for what I had done. I am extremely sorry for what happened to (victim) and to the family and in fact to all the people—all the people of God. I still am very, very sorry and I deeply regret what happened. I also regret this— the terrible shattering it had on my wife and my daughter—all I can do is just say I am sorry.[55]

A letter of support from a psychiatrist attested that Mr. R. "experienced much anguish and remorse that continues to the present day."[56] In the intervening years, Mr. R. had changed vocations, married, become a parent and, according to the court, "was able to restore himself to law abiding productive status."[57]

Meanwhile the complainant also submitted a statement to the court in which he described the psychological and emotional aftermath of these events. He felt alienated from his family and left home to live on the street shortly after contact with Mr. R. had ended. Following an attempted suicide, he was briefly hospitalized. He claimed further that he continues to experience great difficulty in maintaining relationships of intimacy and that his life has involved long-term "anger and depression."[58]

Comparing the two, the judge wrote that the victim had presented as "intelligent, insightful, self-possessed, and articulate. He has accomplished much in the restructuring of his life." Mr. R., on the other hand, presented "as a pitiful, dejected shell of a man who has never forgiven himself for his failure

---

54   ibid [15].
55   ibid [25].
56   ibid [9].
57   ibid [52].
58   ibid [25].

as a Priest. [59] Mr. R. was credited with having feelings of remorse, as expressed and demonstrated, that are "unquestionably genuine and profound."[60] Because of the changes he had made in his life, the judge had concluded, "Institutional incarceration may have originally fit the crime. It no longer fits the criminal."[61] Moreover, the judgment held that he had already made reparation to society by "forging a useful and constructive career."[62] The punishment imposed was that of a conditional sentence in which Mr. R. would be able to remain at home under strict conditions of parole.[63]

The second case involves a man, Mr. C., who was convicted of dangerous driving causing death.[64] Mr. C. was the driver of a vehicle over which he lost control while impaired by alcohol and while driving far in excess of the speed limit. As a result, of the three passengers in his car, one was fatally injured while the driver and the other two passengers received minor injuries. All of the passengers were friends who had worked together for 13 years and who socialized together outside of work.

The judgment describes the defendant as remorseful in these terms:

> Following the accident, he (Mr. C.) suffered deep and long term depression as a result of what had transpired. As he should, he sought medical assistance, he received counseling, and re-received medication to deal with issues of depression. I have no reason to disbelieve his psychiatrist who described him as grief-stricken and depressed. In short, the Defendant is an average law-abiding and productive citizen who made an alcohol-induced error in judgement with tragic result for which the defendant has and will continue to pay dearly. It is, in my opinion … unlikely that the Defendant will ever be free of his financial responsibilities let alone his emotional state.[65]

---

59   ibid [51].

60   ibid [50].

61   ibid [62].

62   ibid [52].

63   A comparatively recent innovation in Canadian sentencing practices at the time this case was decided, the "conditional sentence" is intended to allow certain persons who have been convicted under the criminal code to serve their sentence at home instead of prison. The terms of reference are given in *R. v. Proulx* [2000], 1 S.C.R. [113]: "In determining whether restorative objectives can be satisfied in a particular case, the judge should consider the offender's prospects of rehabilitation; the availability of appropriate community service and treatment programs; whether the offender has acknowledged his or her wrongdoing and expressed remorse …" Under current legislation in Canada, with the passage of the Omnibus Crime Bill—bill C-10 on March 12, 2012, the court would not have been able to impose a conditional sentence for the offence for which Cromien was charged—that of indecent assault.

64   *R. v. Chisholm,* Ontario Ct. of Justice, O.J. 603 [11].

65   ibid [11].

The remorsefulness of the offender was corroborated as well by the immediate family of the victim—wife, mother-in-law, and father-in-law. Before pronouncing sentence, the judge described the defendant in these terms: "He is indeed, aside from his guilty plea, remorseful. I have come to the conclusion and I am convinced beyond a reasonable doubt that evidenced by his mental state and based on the opinion of his psychiatrist and, in fact, his Probation Officer, who is obliged to consider matters such as this, he indeed is remorseful for what he has done."[66]

I take these two judgments not as neutral descriptions of character based on evidence that was submitted but rather as part of a narrative that constitutes how a member of society—one of us as opposed to someone who is a "criminal"— behaves when they have committed a wrongdoing. Whether or not it is the good reputation of the wrongdoer—the "law abidingness" of the one or the "pro-social" characteristics of the other—that imports credibility to the moral performance or the moral performance that confers credibility on their reputation, the remorseful offender is someone who acknowledges without reservation their responsibility, whose suffering is palpable and confirmable both by what is shown and what is corroborated by expert authority, and whose suffering is demonstrated as well by the shame they show at what they have done and by the sacrifices they must make or have made as a result of their wrongdoing. How much of this shame is felt and how much is ritualized is less important than that this is how the court imagines a member of the community in good standing should feel and should act when they have violated communal norms and that remorse and its crediting is what yields the terms by which the character of the offender is corroborated. It is significant that, in the second case, the judge observes that the offender is "aside from his guilty plea, remorseful," which can be taken to suggest that it is not the guilty plea but what accompanies it that validates the offender's claim. The betrayal of community signified by the wrongdoing is redeemed by suffering and sacrifice. Before one can be viewed as not defined by one's crime, as having committed a crime but not therefore a criminal, the offender must demonstrate through sincere self-condemnation marked by shame and the shedding of the offending self—that, through remorse, the self that is loyal to community is more real than the self that has betrayed community.

However, even in cases that fit so fully into the typology of acknowledgment, suffering, and self-transformation, the attribution of remorse is fraught with ambiguity. Appearance and reality are easily reversed so that what seems authentic to one audience can be viewed as strategic by the next. The proximity of law's coercion to the offender's moral performance creates a continuing tension between narrative and counter-narrative. A year after Mr. R.'s conditional sentence, the case was successfully appealed to a higher court that imposed a prison sentence in place of the conditional sentence citing as grounds for their substitution of a more severe punishment, the lower court's "flawed approach to the respondent's

---

66   ibid [21].

remorse."[67] These expressions, it held, were "highly selective and were expressive more of damage control than genuine contrition." It is towards an examination of what might be viewed as the useful or strategic ambiguity of attributions of remorse that I turn in the next section.

Remorse as Seen Through Judicial Discourse

Law's mercy is that which is bestowed upon those who admit their unworthiness and who submit unquestioningly to how their official accuser has defined their wrongdoing. But law's violence is the unspoken contingency in the dialogue on remorse—the offender must be described as if he or she is making a choice that is unconstrained by the ever-present threat of pain and punishment. If the offender shows remorse that can be validated, it is because he (she) actually feels the emotions they are displaying. If the offender fails to offer a convincing demonstration, it is a reflection of what is lacking in his or her character—that he (she) has succumbed to the temptation to act strategically and self-interestedly rather than sincerely and spontaneously or that he (she) simply lacks the capacity to feel remorse. In all instances, the wrongdoer reveals who they are—as either filled with remorse or as rationally manipulating the court to produce the least painful result or as lacking in moral capacity. Never do we encounter the narrative of the offender who is humbled and brought to remorse by fear of the law itself.

But if law's violence is the unnamable condition under which demonstrations of remorse occur, juridical speech gives tacit acknowledgment to the always-tenuous relationship between appearance and reality. Attributions of remorse are invariably contestable and because they are contestable, always provisional. Each of the criteria enunciated above—acknowledgment, suffering, and personal transformation—can be expanded beyond whatever the offender has demonstrated. While a higher court rejected Mr. R.'s claim to remorse, Mr. C.'s claim was also challenged because he had not attended the funeral of his friend nor apologized directly to the family—a challenge that the judge in this case did not accept. Even among those who have been credited with "extreme remorse," such as another offender who is described as experiencing "a great deal of grief and guilt" regarding the act that led to her conviction for Impaired Driving causing death, her claim to remorsefulness is contested by the Crown after learning that she continued to drink after the offence and lied about it. Does this imply that her resolve to change her behavior was half-hearted or insincere or can she still qualify as remorseful because she told the court the truth about her deception when the parole officers were preparing their recommendations?[68] Or in another case, a man who was charged with first-degree murder of his mother is credited by one psychiatrist with feeling remorse because of his "spontaneous and appropriate tears" but challenged by another because his remorse was "variable" and would not necessarily prevent

---

67   *R. v. Cromien* [2002], Ontario Ct. of Appeal, Lexis 72 [6].

68   *R. v. Shore* [2002], Sask. Divisional Ct., Lexis 56, p. 24.

a recurrence.[69] In the majority of cases from the population here analyzed, the judgment mentions that the claims to remorse advanced by the defense were challenged by the prosecution with the court sometimes defending the claim and at other times rejecting it. As compelling as the narrative of acknowledgment, suffering, and personal transformation may be, judicial discourse is permeated by an equally compelling counter-narrative that, no matter how effortful the moral performance, offenders are ultimately ruled less by conscience than by self-interest. The coexistence of these two narratives together with the aforementioned flexibility in how the criteria for identifying remorse are applied are what make the designation ambiguous and provisional. The construing of Mr. R. as remorseful, and the subsequent revocation of this judgment, is simply an exaggerated instance of a more pervasive tendency to expand or diminish the criteria for remorse in support or in opposition to a particular outcome.

But this is not to suggest that such ambiguity leads to a randomness of results or that it is without its uses. It is this variability in elaboration that allows other contingencies to enter into judicial discourse. Under the rubric of remorse as acknowledgment, the court can demand of the offender not just a guilty plea but verbatim agreement with the terms of the charge as well as proactive efforts to communicate this acknowledgment to the victim. In the context of remorse as suffering for the other, the court can expect not just the expression of grief but feelings of devastation—not just an attempt at suicide but a clear indication that such acts of self-destruction spring from empathy with the other and not from fear of consequences. As for remorse as self-transformation, the court can demand proof of a major characterological change rather than a mere willingness by offenders to allow themselves to be changed.

At one level, the most obvious contingency is the gravity of the offence—those offences that are accorded longer sentences are also the same offences for which there is more contestation as well as expanded expectations. But the thrust of this analysis is to suggest that juridical speech does not merely respond to what are more serious offences by adding more conditions for claims of remorse to be validated. Judgments about remorse are not just reactive. They are constitutive, they establish the gravity of the offence by defining how much suffering, how much submission, and how drastic a self-transformation is required for the offender to reestablish themselves as a member of the moral community. For the crime for which Mr. R. was convicted, the price of membership—the pain threshold by which remorse is measured—just increased. It is in these terms that one can speak of a moral economy of suffering.

If the remorseful offender is the recipient of law's mercy as well as the court's approbation as someone who is still a member of the moral community—"not inherently bad" to quote from one judgment—the obverse is the denunciation of those who do not show remorse coupled with the withdrawal of mercy. Those who do not accept responsibility, who do not suffer for their transgressions, who do

---

69   *R. v. W.G.F.* [2003], Ontario Superior Ct. of Justice, Lexis 663 [4].

not evince a willingness to alter their character are not merely disfavored—they are the objects of judicial outrage. The language directed towards such persons who are described as having shown "not one scintilla of remorse" or "flagrant contempt (by) not showing any ... remorse or acknowledgment of wrongdoing,"[70] both constitutes and reflects the vast moral divide between those who are worthy of law's mercy and those who are not.

But the thrust of the foregoing analysis is not just that juridical discourse constitutes when remorse should be demonstrated but how it should be demonstrated. Through other discursive lenses, it might be important to decide whether feelings of remorse derived from the adverse judgments of the community or from falling short of one's own moral standards[71] or whether attempts at suicide or self-infliction of pain or other demonstrations of visible suffering are too self-referential to qualify as expressions of an emotion such as remorse that should be focused more on the victim than on the self. Through the prospect of mercy and moral accreditation but also the concealed threat of violence, judicial discourse shapes the content of remorse in a way that reflects the context in which it is produced. If it is appreciated that remorse is not just a psychological trait inherent in the individual but rather an attribute that is situated in a specific social context, the impact of juridical discourse on the shaping of remorse becomes all the more comprehensible. The form in which remorse must be expressed is that of submission to a greater power- the moral performances that are validated all have as their common point of reference a posture of abjection and surrender by the offender before the authority of the law. Whether or not these manifestations correspond to actual feelings of shame or guilt, in the population of cases here considered, it is clear that, in extended contests, anything short of unconditional acknowledgment of wrongdoing coupled with severe self-condemnation will not lead to the conferring of the law's mercy. At the same time, no act engenders greater outrage from the court than outright defiance in which the offender admits responsibility for the act but is indifferent to its wrongfulness. The charge of "flagrant contempt" cited above is for practicing law without having the proper qualifications. Outrage at the absence of remorse has far less to do with the gravity of the offence than with the lack of deference that such a stance communicates. Along with the other requisites for a successful moral performance, remorseful offenders must show that they know their place.

By attending to the remorsefulness of the offender and by taking into account its presence or absence, legal discourse comes to link act to character and doing to being. The modern trial or tribunal hearing is a proceeding consisting of two phases. In the first of these phases, the court or adjudicator make a finding of whether the person is culpable or responsible for the misconduct that has been alleged. In the second phase, it is the character of the offender that is in question—

---

70   *Law Society of British Columbia v. Hanson* [2004], BC Supreme Ct., Lexis 1341 [48].

71   Taylor (1985), p. 98; Tudor (2001), p. 127.

whether or not they are the kinds of person who are likely to commit the offense for which they have been convicted. Remorse is the attribute by which this linkage between act and character is achieved. But nowhere is the signifying power of the category of remorse more amply demonstrated than in the life and death struggle over representation that is the hallmark of the contemporary American capital trial in which juries are asked to decide between a life sentence without parole and the death penalty. How designation as remorseful or remorseless is used to mobilize the sentiments of jurors in support or opposition to the ultimate punishment is the subject of Chapter 3.

Chapter 3

Making Monsters: Contemporary Uses of the Pathological Approach to Remorse[1]

If, as one writer has recently suggested, the criminal trial has from its inception served as a veritable theater of contrition[2] in which defendants come before court and community with humility and remorse, perhaps, in no other legal arena is this drama enacted with greater intensity than in the modern bifurcated American capital trial. If the first phase of the capital trial addresses the familiar questions of culpability and intent, the second phase includes as part of its ambit not just the enumerated aggravating and mitigating factors that are more or less replicated in each of the states in which capital punishment is permitted but what is more loosely described as considerations of character. It is in this second phase that the jury that has already decided in favor of conviction for a capital crime reconvenes and decides between life without parole or death by execution.

But the reactions of jurors in this penalty phase do not take place in a vacuum.[3] How the character of the offender is perceived is shaped by the narratives and counter-narratives that are entered, or allowed entry, into the legal forum. The task of the prosecutor is to somehow convince the jury that life without parole is an insufficient response to the crime that has been perpetrated despite the full protection from danger that such a punishment arguably affords. The defense, on the other hand, must craft a portrait of the offender that separates what is often the most chilling of transgressions from the persons who committed them.[4]

In light of our aforementioned discussion then, it is hardly surprising that attributions of remorse should figure so prominently in the dueling rhetoric with

---

1 This chapter is a revised and updated version of an earlier article, Richard Weisman, "Remorse and Psychopathy at the Penalty Phase of the Capital Trial—How Psychiatry's View of 'Moral Insanity' Helps Build the Case for Death," in Austin Sarat, ed., *Studies in Law, Society, and Politics*, Vol. 41, 2008, pp. 187–217.

2 Sadakat Kadri, *The Trial: A History from Socrates to O.J. Simpson*, Random House, New York, 2005, pp. 213–214.

3 In order to protect jurors' confidentiality, the responses of jurors in the National Capital Jury Project mentioned above could not be analyzed in relation to specific trials. Hence we do not know from the research how jurors' perceptions of the defendant's remorse might have been shaped by the details of the crime or by how he or she was portrayed by prosecution, defense, or other witnesses.

4 One of the most penetrating analyses of how narratives are inserted into the penalty phase of the capital trial is still Austin Sarat, "Speaking of Death: Narratives of Violence in Capital Trials". *Law and Society Review 27*, 1993, pp. 19–58.

which the death-qualified jury is confronted. The offender who fails to demonstrate remorse after conviction for an atrocious crime can all the more easily be expelled from the moral community and, with this expulsion, forfeit the goodwill and empathic identification that membership provides.[5] The chief prosecutor in the penalty phase of the trial of McVeigh did not neglect to add this significant detail to his characterization of the offender, "Not a single witness testified at any other time that Timothy McVeigh ever had a tear in his eye except when he was concerned about his own welfare, except when he was concerned and worried about his own death."[6]

But there are few Meursaults in the penalty phase of the capital trial. Apart from those who claim to have been wrongly convicted or perhaps, like McVeigh, act from political conviction as we shall discuss in the next chapter, most offenders endeavor to present themselves as remorseful or, at the very least, as not unremorseful. It is in this sense that the modern trial for capital punishment involves a life and death struggle over how remorse is performed and whether the performance will be credited or discredited. One of the objectives of this chapter is to draw from a recent population of capital cases to show how attributions of remorse or its absence are deployed to build an identity for the capital offender to persuade jurors to choose between life and death.

This analysis would remain incomplete, however, without consideration of one of the most significant developments in the modern judicial approach to the remorseless perpetrator. In this approach, the absence of remorse becomes not merely a breach of expectations that invites severe moral condemnation but a symptom of an underlying pathology that marks the wrongdoer as variously diseased, impaired, or otherwise incapable of feeling what a normal member of the community would feel under similar circumstances. In the first section, I discuss the history of this shift not in order to document the gradual, circuitous evolution from the early nineteenth-century category of moral insanity to the contemporary diagnoses of psychopathy and antisocial personality disorder as much as to place in historical relief the particular configuration of assumptions by which remorse and pathology are currently associated. Once I have identified the distinctive way in which the absence of remorse is pathologized in contemporary medical-psychological discourse, it then becomes possible to show more clearly how this approach has been translated from its uncertain and tenuous status within forensic psychology and psychiatry to its currently ambiguous and controversial status in American law.

---

5 Garvey captures these strong sentiments when he writes that jurors are "apt to respond to the remorseful defendant not only with good will but also *without fear and disgust*, both of which tended to recede in the face of the defendant's remorse" in "The Emotional Economy of Capital Sentencing," *New York University Law Review* 75 (2000), pp. 58–59. [my emphasis].

6 *Westlaw 312609*, 1997, (D. Colo. trans. Para 32).

In the second section of this chapter, I hope to bring out the representations of the remorseless offender that help to promote the intense moral indignation sufficient to decide in favor of death when life without parole is the only other option. Here I will focus on the critical contribution of the pathological approach both in framing how the feelings of the capital offender are to be interpreted and in supplying a rationale for death as the appropriate punishment. In developing this analysis, I have built upon and modified the classic formulation of the ritual of public denunciation culminating in dehumanization offered by Harold Garfinkel.[7]

My primary objective is to look at what the absence of remorse comes to symbolize about the wrongdoer and the consequences of identifying the act with the person. I want to show how the casting of wrongdoers as without remorse separates them from the community not just by virtue of their transgression, but also by the purported personal qualities that are embodied in the act. The pathological approach to remorse widens even further the difference between those who show remorse and those who do not even as it enlarges the population to whom the designation of remorselessness can be applied. Here the disregard of feeling rules embodied by the refusal or incapacity to express remorse is not only condemned for its rejection of the moral-emotive foundation of community but also naturalized as a psychobiological condition from which the wrongdoer cannot be rehabilitated. It is this explosive combination of moral condemnation and medical pessimism that gives added justification for imposing on the psychopathic perpetrator the gravest sanctions available in US law. That the term "monster" is often used as a substitute for "psychopath" or "sociopath" in modern cultural iconography should not surprise us in view of how persons placed in these categories have been characterized.[8]

Remorse, Psychopathology, and the Law—Building the Framework for Interpretation

From Affliction to Abnormality

In 1826, in his *Discussions medico-legale pour Henriette Cornier,*[9] Dr. Etienne Georget, a French physician and one of the forerunners of modern forensic

---

7 Harold Garfinkel, "Conditions of Successful Degradation Ceremonies," *American Journal of Sociology* 61 (1956), pp. 420–424.

8 See Russell D. Covey, "Criminal Madness: Cultural Iconography and Insanity," (2009) 61 *Stanford L.R.*, especially pp. 1413–1427, for emergence of psychopathic killer as the modern icon of the monster, as someone who is dangerous, irrational, manipulative, and resistant to change either through imprisonment or therapy. To which I would add as a defining feature—the notion of psychopathy as biological abnormality.

9 Etienne Georget (1826), *Discussions medico-legale pour Henriette Cormier*. Paris: Migneret, pp. 71–130.

psychiatry, reported on a case that occurred in Paris and that would be retold in England, the United States, and elsewhere in nineteenth-century Europe as representing a turning point in the history of mental disorder and the interrelationship between law and psychiatry. What was so remarkable and anomalous about Henriette Cornier was not her atrocious act of violence but the impossibility of making sense of it within the legal, medical, or psychological frameworks then available. One day, after a "singular change was observed in her character,"[10] Cornier, a 27-year-old servant, left her place of employment to visit a neighboring shop to buy some cheese for the family where she resided. She had always shown affection for the shopkeeper's daughter and so was able to persuade her to entrust her with the child for a walk. She then took the child back to her mistress's house, and, laying her across her own bed, severed the child's head with a kitchen knife. She was reported later to have felt no particular emotion—"without remorse or grief" in the original narrative as well as in subsequent published accounts— during the commission of this deed. When the mother came for her child some two hours later, Cornier informed her that: "Your child is dead." The mother who did not at first believe her entered the chamber where she was confronted with "the bloody sight of the mutilated fragments of her child."[11] At that point, Cornier picked up the head of the murdered child, and threw it into the street from the open window. Why did she do this, she was later asked? She replied that she wanted to attract public attention so that people might come up to her room and see that she alone was responsible for the murder.[12]

I dwell on this case because it constituted the first time a court in Europe or North America was asked to consider as a defense to criminal culpability a new category of insanity for which the primary symptom was the criminal act itself. Because Cornier demonstrated no defects in cognition—she understood the consequences of her action and was fully aware that it violated the laws of her community—she did not belong in the more familiar category of "insane" perpetrators who committed crimes in a state of delirium or who exhibited other signs of cognitive disorientation. At the same time, because the prosecution could establish no motive for her behavior that was intelligible to contemporaries—no prior history of grievance with the family of her victim to build a narrative of revenge and no hope of personal gain consistent with any instrumental objective—

---

10   See accounts by Isaac Ray (1838), *Treatise on the medical jurisprudence of insanity.* Boston, M.A., Charles C. Little and James Brown, pp. 219–222, and James Cowles Prichard (1842), *On the different forms of insanity in relation to jurisprudence.* London: Hippolyte Balliere, pp. 95–102, for the most influential of the many contemporary accounts. See also Michel Foucault (2003), *Abnormal—Lectures at the College de France, 1974–1975.* G. Burchell, (Trans.) New York: Picador, pp. 112–134 for highly informative discussion and analysis of case.

11   Ray (n 10) p. 220.

12   *"Pour qu'on fut bien assure en montant dans la chamber qu'elle seule etait coupable,"* Georget, 1826, p. 79.

her act of violence could not be situated within the conventional parameters of willful criminal misconduct. Cornier presented the anomaly of someone who "knew" that her act was immoral and unlawful and yet could offer no motive for why she had done it. As viewed by her contemporaries, the only evidence of insanity in this "lucid" perpetrator was what she had done.

A decade after this much discussed trial, leading Anglo-American interpreters of the link between law and madness were still debating how to understand and categorize her affliction in the language of the faculty psychology of the period.[13] Was it a form of moral insanity, "a perversion of natural feelings, affections, inclinations, temper, habits, and moral dispositions without any notable lesions of the intellect or knowing and reasoning faculties, and particularly without any maniacal hallucination?"[14] Or was it a disease of the will—a form of homicidal madness—in which the perpetrator demonstrated a fatal incapacity to resist her homicidal urges, as James Cowles Prichard would suggest?[15] But regardless of which faculty was affected—that of the feelings or the will—it was already clear to contemporaries that expanding the insanity defense to include those who were not cognitively impaired when they committed their wrongdoing constituted a major redrawing of the boundaries of responsibility with sweeping implications for criminal law. How would one now distinguish the cognitively unimpaired murderer whose actions were willful and deliberate from the cognitively unimpaired insane offender whose wrongdoings were caused by their affliction? It is in the crafting of this distinction that we can discern the vast changes that occurred during the nineteenth century in how the lucid perpetrator would be portrayed.

Early commentaries would describe Cornier whether as morally insane, or as afflicted with homicidal madness as radically different from those who belonged in the category of criminally culpable offenders. As Isaac Ray would write in 1838, the Corniers of this world were not to be classed among those who were depraved or perverse—instead, such persons had characters that were "mild and peaceable, and their days were spent in the quiet and creditable discharge of the duties belonging to their station, till a cloud of melancholy enveloped their minds, and … they

---

13　The dominant school of psychology in the early nineteenth century held that the mind could be divided into the separate faculties of will, feeling, and intellect, and that each of these faculties operated independently of the other two—see S.A. Rippa (1992), *Education in a Free Society: An American History* (7th edition), New York, Longman.

14　Ray (n 10) pp. 169–170. Ray is quoting from Prichard's definition of moral insanity, which in turn he subdivided into "general moral mania" and "partial moral mania" [my emphasis]. If the derangement was manifested in all the affective faculties, it fell into the former category; if it was confined to "one or a few of the affective faculties"(p. 180), as in the case of Cornier—she was insane only when she committed the act—then it fell into the latter category.

15　Prichard (n 10) pp. 19–20; 93, 95. It may reflect the imprecision of these categories that Prichard, who had introduced the concept of moral insanity, categorized Cornier's affliction as a disease of the will whereas Ray, borrowing from Prichard, considered her affliction to be a derangement in the faculty that controlled feelings.

perpetrated a single deed the very thought of which they would have previously shuddered with horror."[16] What precipitated the atrocious act was a striking change in the conduct of the individual signaling the onset of the pathology—or, as Foucault would describe Cornier's defense at her trial—"a crack appears and there is no resemblance between the act and the person."[17] The atrocious act would cast no reflection on Cornier's character, only on her pathology.

Even her lack of grief and remorse for so horrifying an act, however "unnatural," was not the same absence of appropriate affect as that which would be exhibited by the true murderer. While Cornier had shown no emotion when her homicidal act was revealed, this was consistent with her "*manie sans delire.*" As Esquirol[18] had written in a passage quoted by both Ray and Prichard, "the homicidal monomaniac[19] testifies neither remorse nor repentance, nor satisfaction, and, if judicially condemned, perhaps acknowledges the justice of the sentence."[20] Cornier, for example, made no effort to escape custody nor to evade responsibility for her actions—not only did she make it clear that she alone perpetrated the deed but her comment to the magistrate during her examination was that she knew her crime deserved death and that she desired it.[21] "This deserves the death penalty." On the other hand, Ray continued, "the criminal either denies or confesses his guilt: if the latter, he either humbly sues for mercy, or glories in his crimes, and leaves the world cursing his judges and with his last breath exclaiming against the injustice of his fate."[22] The murderer who kills willfully may repent of his crime but only for the ulterior purpose of obtaining a mercy that is undeserved. When he or she is finally sent to their execution, their criminal character will once again be demonstrated through their anger and defiance.

Whether afflicted with homicidal madness or with moral mania, Henriette Cornier committed an act that shocked the sensibilities of her contemporaries. Her brutal decapitation of her infant victim was discussed on both sides of the Atlantic. Yet, at this earliest stage of formulation, the lucid but insane perpetrator is still entitled to a measure of the same solicitude and exemptions that are granted to those afflicted with other illnesses—treatment rather than punishment was the

---

16   Ray (n 10) p. 275

17   Foucault (n 10) p. 127.

18   J.E.D. Esquirol, (1722–95), who was a founder of clinical psychiatry, along with Philippe Pinel, and one of Etienne Georget's teachers.

19   Early nineteenth-century French psychiatric nosology grouped both those who were cognitively disoriented and those whose mental disorder centered on the emotions in the same category of *monomania* whereas the Anglo-American approach was to confine monomania to delusional thinking while placing affective disorder without cognitive defect in a separate category—that of moral insanity following Prichard pp. 36–61; or "moral mania," following Ray (pp. 168–170). For a relatively clear formulation of these distinctions, see *Report of the Metropolitan Commissioners in Lunacy*, London, 1844.

20   Ray (n 10) p. 232.

21   ibid p. 221; Foucault (n 10) p. 125.

22   Ray (n 10) p. 232.

remedy even if there was no likelihood of release from detention for acts of such brutality. In the accounts at trial as offered by the physicians for the defense and in the later commentaries, Cornier is described as herself a victim of her affliction—she is portrayed by Ray when on trial as trembling, melancholic, and in "profound chagrin."[23] As Prichard would suggest about the morally insane, "such persons must be admitted to be morally guilty and to deserve to suffer. But the calamity with which we know them to be afflicted is already so great, that humanity forbids our entertaining the thought of adding to it."[24] In this early representation of the cognitively lucid but insane transgressor, where the act, however despicable, does not define the person and where the perpetrator's being is still separated from their doing, there lingers the perception that but for their affliction, such persons are not so different in terms of how they feel about what they did from the rest of the community.

Yet, by the early twentieth century, the cognitively unimpaired insane offender now firmly incorporated within the category of the "morally insane" would be reconceived in ways that would be much closer to contemporary formulations. Richard von Krafft-Ebing's *Text-book of Insanity*, one of the most widely disseminated manuals of forensic medicine and psychiatry, originally published in 1875 in the first of four German editions—finally translated into English in 1905—and cited as one of the defining texts on insanity by English and American medical and legal authorities well exemplifies the changes that occurred in the intervening 50 years.[25] Profoundly influenced by the biological and evolutionist turn in psychiatry and early criminology,[26] Krafft-Ebing's work reformulates moral insanity less as an illness that is transitory than as a condition that at its worst and most frequent, is hereditary and organic, and at best, is acquired as the result of other neurologically based mental defects. In the former case, the prognosis is hopeless incurability—in the later, successful removal of the mental defect may result in remission of the abnormality.[27]

More importantly, the wrongdoing of the morally insane, whether criminal or otherwise, is conceived as a true expression of their underlying personality—"moral insanity affects the innermost nucleus of the individuality in its emotional, ethical, and moral relations."[28] What radically distinguishes those who have this

23 ibid pp. 221–222.

24 Prichard (n 10) p. 178.

25 Dr. Richard von Krafft-Ebing's *Text-book of Insanity, Based on Clinical Observations,* 1905. Krafft-Ebing's clinical insights on moral insanity are cited by Havelock Ellis, 1890, *The Criminal,* London: Walter Scott, p. 229, and by Enrico Fermi, 1897, *Criminal Sociology*, New York: P. Appleton and Company, p. 26, among others.

26 For useful overview of shift in meaning of category, see Nicole Rafter, "The Unrepentant Horse-Slasher: Moral Insanity and the Origins of Criminological Thought," *Criminology* 42 (2004), pp. 979–1007.

27 Krafft-Ebing, p. 625.

28 ibid p. 622.

condition is what Krafft-Ebing calls a "more or less complete moral insensibility,"[29] by which he means that even when the morally insane are conscious of moral standards, they lack the feelings and affects that engender commitment to these standards. The best they can do is memorize the rules and codes, "but if they enter consciousness they remain uncolored by feeling and affects and are dead ideas." At their core, persons who fall into this category are unable to experience or demonstrate the feelings that come naturally to persons with normal "social instincts" as evidenced by their "coldness of heart, their indifference to the lot of their nearest relatives, (their absence) of scruples of conscience or repentance."[30] By recasting moral insanity as no longer merely an illness but as a congenital abnormality that penetrates to the nucleus of the person, the wrongful deeds of the morally insane have become an expression of their essence. In this new approach to moral insanity, act and person are now shown to correspond.

How then is the morally insane wrongdoer to be distinguished from the willful criminal if repeated and incorrigible wrongdoing is one of the primary manifestations? Here, Krafft-Ebing suggests that their "moral blindness" fails them even in their criminal pursuits. For here, their lack of judgment makes them astonishingly negligent, lacking in the "most elementary rules of prudence in committing their criminal acts." Just as the morally insane are not able to conform their conduct to legal restrictions, they are also not free to obey these restrictions— unlike the putatively rational criminal, they are unable to prevent themselves from engaging in "strange, immoral, or criminal acts."[31] Their defiance of the law and their proclivity to immoral behavior differ from criminal misconduct because these tendencies are so unrestrained, so ruthless, and so contrary to their criminal purpose of benefiting from their ill-gotten gains.

In Krafft-Ebing's work, the descriptions of the morally insane reveal a stance towards the pathology that is different in tone and orientation from all the other case studies that are included in the volume. For each of these other illnesses, conditions, or impairments, no matter how transgressive the symptom, the patient is viewed as suffering from or otherwise adversely affected by their affliction. It is only when we turn to the morally insane that the language shifts to one of severe moral condemnation devoid of compassion for the offending pathology. The woman whom Krafft-Ebing uses to illustrate the abnormality is described as "impossible, very irritable, unsocial, coarse and without feeling, and inciting other patients to disobey hospital regulations."[32] What is mentioned is not how she has suffered from her condition but how the interpersonal and behavioral manifestations of her condition have adversely affected others. At the end of the case, it is noted that she was transferred to an institution for the chronic insane— that she has been judged incurable. By the time of Krafft-Ebing's work, moral

---

29   ibid p. 623.
30   ibid.
31   ibid p. 625.
32   ibid p. 626.

insanity has been transformed from an affliction from which one suffers and which might well be temporary to an abnormality that is hereditary, untreatable, and a continuing source of danger to others. As his prescription for dealing with the condition, Krafft-Ebing writes, "these savages in society must be kept in asylums for their own and the safety of society."[33] The morally insane wrongdoer has become less someone entitled to exemptions from criminal responsibility than one from whom the community needs protection. As we shall see, it is a version of this representation that is reflected in the contemporary understanding of those classed as manifesting psychopathic disorder or antisocial personality disorder who also engage in criminal wrongdoing, who are cognitively intact, and who are perceived as incapable of feeling remorse.

Contemporary Representations of Remorselessness as Pathology

In the 2000 edition of the DSM, (DSM IV TR, 2000), the first criterion for the diagnosis of antisocial personality disorder specifies "a pervasive pattern of disregard for and violation of the rights of others since age 15 years, as indicated by three or more of seven factors among which is included 'lack of remorse,' as indicated by being indifferent to or rationalizing having hurt, mistreated, or stolen from another."[34] But just as the absence of remorse serves as one of the indications of antisocial personality disorder and psychopathy, so also the meaning of this absence can only be understood in the context of these psychiatric constructs. For present purposes, I will treat the categories of antisocial personality and psychopathy as interchangeable in conformity with what I take to be contemporary usage. Despite efforts by some to confine antisocial personality disorder to what is behavioral and descriptive as distinct from psychopathy which focuses as well on those elements of character that require a greater degree of interpretation,[35] the two dimensions of the disorder—behavioral and characterological—are intermeshed not only in *DSM IV-TR* but in much of the current literature for both categories. One further caveat—I use the term representation in full recognition that this is not how authors of texts in forensic psychiatry would refer to their clinical insights and observations—my purpose in applying this concept is to bring out the interpretive work that is involved in developing these formulations while bracketing their correspondence to veridical reality. I believe that historical shifts in perception as well as contemporary debates over the validity of the category justify this

---

33   ibid.

34   *DSM IV-TR,* 2000, p. 706.

35   Hare, R. D. (1996), "Psychopathy and Antisocial Personality Disorder: A case of Diagnostic Confusion" *Psychiatric Times,* 13(2), pp. 1–4. E-journal at <http://www. psychiatrictimes.com/p960239.html> accessed November 2, 2012.

bracketing of reality by demonstrating that there is variation in interpretation and therefore interpretive choice or agency in how to formulate the construct.[36]

As indicated above, the chief defining feature of psychopathy and its antecedents is engagement in transgressive behavior with full cognitive awareness of both the wrongfulness of the conduct and the likelihood of moral-communal condemnation. Within this larger context, for all the changes that have occurred since Krafft-Ebing's work with regard to etiology, nosology, and theories of psychopathology, at the level of clinical description, there are important similarities in what the lack of remorse has come to signify about persons placed in these categories. Most important is the perception that the legal and moral wrongdoing of persons so diagnosed, are linked inextricably to deeply rooted and relatively unalterable personality traits. Whether in influential specialized texts such as Hervey Cleckley's *Mask of Sanity—An Attempt to Clarify Some Issues about the Psychopathic Personality*, reprinted in five editions between 1941 and 1982, or in more popularly oriented works such as Robert Hare's *Without Conscience—The Disturbing World of Psychopaths Among Us*, or Martha Stout's *The Sociopath Next Door*,[37] the psychopath is someone whose irresponsible, destructive behavior is fully consistent with and inseparable from what Hare has referred to as the interpersonal and affective features of the condition. The examples and illustrations contained in all these works make it clear that the harm that the psychopath inflicts on others whether through material or emotional exploitation or any other form of violence is strategic, deliberate, and that the psychopath as perpetrator is at least intellectually cognizant of the relationship between action and consequence. But what is emphasized in contemporary formulations is that while the troublesomeness of the psychopath may be manifested in behavioral transgressions, the disturbance is primarily characterological. If social deviance may be one highly visible way in which the disturbance reveals itself, the core of the pathology lies in deeply rooted character traits of the individual. For the psychopath, action is a reflection of being.[38]

---

36   For examples of this approach to the analysis of psychopathy as social category, see Michael Petrunik and Richard Weisman, "Constructing Joseph Fredericks: Competing Narratives of a Child Sex Murderer," 28 (2005), *International Journal of Law and Psychiatry*, pp. 75–96, and Cary Federman, Dave Holmes, and Jean Daniel Jacob, "Deconstructing the Psychopath: A Critical Discursive Analysis," *Cultural Critique* 72 (Spring, 2009), pp. 36–65.

37   Robert D. Hare, *Without Conscience—The Disturbing World of Psychopaths,* New York: Guilford Press, 1999; Martha Stout, *The Sociopath Next Door,* New York: Broadway Books, 2005.

38   See, for example, the opening sentence in Hare, "Psychopathy, Affect, and Behavior," in D. Cooke et al., eds, *Psychopathy: Theory, Research, and Implications for Society*, pp. 105–124, Norwell, MA, Kluwer, Academic Publications, 1998,—"Psychopathy is a socially devastating personality disorder defined by a constellation of affective, interpersonal, and behavioral characteristics, including egocentricity, manipulativeness, deceitfulness, lack of empathy, guilt or remorse, and a propensity to violate social and legal expectations and norms." Affective, interpersonal, and behavioral characteristics all

In what then does the disturbance identified by Cleckley, Hare, and others consist? Psychopathy is first and foremost an affective disorder—an abnormality that results in an incapacity to feel or experience emotions in a way that is central to interpersonal relations. It is as if the entire spectrum of human emotions is truncated to the point that the psychopath has access only to the most shallow and superficial of feelings, whether it be anger, love, fear, or hatred.[39] But the primary locus of the deficiency is in what moral philosophers have referred to as the moral emotions or those emotions that promote or maintain ethical conduct towards others. The psychopath is someone who lacks remorse, guilt, or shame for the harm that he or she may inflict on others, feels no empathy for the suffering that he has caused, and refuses to accept responsibility for any wrongdoing. While these are separate items in the clinical profile offered by Cleckley and in the *Psychopathy Check List Revised* as developed by Hare,[40] all point to the inability of the psychopath to experience from within the feelings that restrain exploitative and callous behavior towards others. At the deepest level of character—beneath what is expressed in public—the psychopath lacks the emotive ability or capacity to attach himself to others or to the moral codes that sustain communal life.

Equally significant to the modern representation of psychopathy is its intractability as indicated by both its severity and its resistance to treatment. Cleckley's central metaphor for psychopathy—given in the title of his book, *The Mask of Sanity*—is grounded in the paradox of appearance and reality. The condition that most resembles normality in its outward manifestations—the psychopath lacks even the social awkwardness and nervousness of the neurotic— is in actuality the condition with the most devastating prognosis.[41] Just as the least visible of aphasic disorders—semantic aphasia—is also the most disabling, the

---

contribute to the disorder. Indeed, the tendency to equate personality disorders such as psychopathy or anti-social personality with social deviance has been sharply criticized by another important contributor to modern formulations of the category. Theodore Millon writes in Millon, *Disorders of Personality, DSM-IV and Beyond*, 1996 (2nd edition), New York: John Wiley and Sons, p. 429, that "I have never felt comfortable with the write-up for the antisocial personality disorder. I very much agree with those who contend that the focus given is oriented too much the 'criminal personality' and not sufficiently towards those who have avoided criminal involvements."

39   For example, in Hervey M. Cleckley, *The Mask of Sanity*, 5th edition, C.V. Mosby and Co.: St. Louis, 1976, p. 260, the author writes in answer to the question of what ultimately distinguishes the psychopath for those with other mental disorders: " My concept of the psychopath's functioning postulates a selective defect or elimination which prevents important components of normal experience from being integrated into the whole human reaction, particularly an elimination or attenuation of "those strong affective components that ordinarily arise in major personal and social issues. " [my emphasis].

40   Hare (1998), p. 106.

41   Cleckley, p. 383: "His mask is that of robust mental health. Yet he has a disorder that often manifests itself in conduct far more seriously abnormal than that of the schizophrenic."

psychopath, for all his skill at mimicking sanity, is afflicted with a disturbance as intransigent and encompassing as those with the most obvious symptoms of psychological disorder. Adding to the gravity of the condition is its incurability. With few exceptions in the current literature, psychopathy is represented as a condition with an early onset that is virtually unresponsive to any of the treatment modalities currently available. Nor do the persons who fall into this category generally volunteer to be treated thereby worsening an already dismal prognosis. The therapeutic pessimism expressed by Krafft-Ebing in his case study of moral insanity is thus closely paralleled by the despairing prognosis offered for persons diagnosed with psychopathy or antisocial personality disorder today.[42] Contributing further to this pessimism is the elision of the social as a significant factor in the etiology of the condition. Clinical profiles portray persons with these conditions as demographically diverse—unaffected by considerations of class and status—and as likely to grow up in well-functioning loving families as in families with severe dysfunction.[43] Indeed, the thrust of much of contemporary research is towards naturalizing psychopathy as a condition that is correlated with physiological and neurological differences and potentially traceable to bio-genetic causes[44] As one widely cited text describes it, "I would hypothesize that the term reptilian state describes the psychobiology of certain, primary, psychopathic characters."[45] This casting of the psychopath into biological otherness creates an even sharper boundary between psychopathy and normality even as it strengthens the case for therapeutic pessimism.

Yet, for all the gravity of the abnormality, its recalcitrance to change, and its possible biological causation, psychopathy is evaluated as a condition that should not entitle those so designated to an exemption from criminal responsibility. Both Cleckley and Hare, for example, assert that the incapacities of the psychopath—

---

42   As described in B.A. Arrigo and S. Shipley, "The confusion over psychopathy (I): Historical Considerations, 45, *International Journal of Offender Therapy and Comparative Criminology* (2001), pp. 325–344, see especially pp. 328–329. One of the most influential and frequently cited studies supporting therapeutic pessimism is still Grant T. Harris, Marnie E. Rice, and Catherine A. Cormier, 15(6) *Law and Human Behavior,* 1991, pp. 625–637.

43   For example, Cleckley writes: "A very large percentage of the psychopaths I have studied show backgrounds that appear conducive to happy development and excellent adjustment." 1976, p. 410. See also Hare, 1999, pp. 174–175, "We found no evidence that the family backgrounds of psychopaths differ from those of other criminals." Or regarding the onset of psychopathy, Hare observes: "In sharp contrast (to other criminals) the quality of family life had absolutely no effect on the emergence of criminality in psychopaths. Whether the family life was stable or unstable, psychopaths first appeared in adult court at an average age of 14 (p. 175)."

44   See, for example, J. Blair, D. Mitchell, and K. Blair, *The Psychopath: Emotion and the Brain.* Malden, Mass: Blackwell, 2005; A. Abbott (March 15, 2001). "Into the mind of a killer." *Nature,* 410, pp. 296–298; Hare (n.38).

45   J. Reid Meloy, *The Psychopathic Mind: Origins, Dynamics, and Treatment,* Rowman and Littlefield, 2004, p. 69.

however resistant to change—do not negate the ability to make choices and weigh consequences.[46] But if the psychopath is someone who can make choices and who is nonetheless likely to engage in criminal wrongdoing, what is the difference between willful misconduct that is a manifestation of psychopathy and willful misconduct that is merely criminal and non-pathological? In an argument reminiscent of Krafft-Ebing, both authors, among others, suggest that there is a non-instrumental purposelessness to the criminal misconduct committed by psychopathic offenders in contrast to those who are non-psychopathic, and that, unlike those not so afflicted, they are unable to learn from experience. Indeed, Hare goes so far as to urge a rigorous separation between those who exhibit only the behavioral manifestations associated with psychopathy (heretofore to be designated as antisocial personality disorder) and those who in addition demonstrate the affective and interpersonal dimension of the disorder lest they who have only antisocial personality disorder be unfairly ascribed the dismal prognosis of the true psychopath.[47] Hence, the criminality of the psychopath is if anything more virulent, less purposeful, and less susceptible to control through punishment than that of non-psychopathic offenders even though both are credited with free will.

The final piece in the modern representation of the psychopath is perhaps the most significant in terms of the role of remorse. Unlike the late nineteenth- and early twentieth-century conceptions, the middle to late twentieth century has reconfigured the psychopath as the consummate social performer.[48] Indeed, one

---

46   Cleckley (1976), pp. 423–424, maintained this position through to the last edition of his work: "For many years, I have consistently tried to emphasize my strong conviction that psychopaths should not be regarded as psychotic in the sense of being 'innocent because of insanity' of the wrongs they do ... Whatever in the psychotic patient there is that may render him not responsible, or less than normally responsible, for crime, cannot, in my opinion, be found in the psychopath's defect." Or, similarly Hare (1993, p. 143) writes: "In my opinion, psychopaths certainly know enough about what they are doing to be held accountable for their actions." For a recent judicial endorsement of this position, see *People v. Castenada,* Supreme Court of California [2011] 254 P. 3rd at p. 291 where in rejecting the argument by the defendant that his diagnosis of antisocial personality disorder could be used as a mental disability in mitigation of the death penalty, the court wrote: "First, there is no objective evidence the society views as inappropriate the execution of death-eligible individuals who have antisocial personality disorder. Second, although the expert testimony reflected that individuals with an antisocial personality disorder are not amenable to treatment, the evidence also reflected that such individuals are aware of what they are doing, and that they have the ability to choose not to commit crimes. Accordingly, the disorder does not diminish their criminal culpability."

47   Hare (n 35).

48   On the remarkable abilities of the psychopath, Cleckley writes: "Not only can he (perhaps involuntarily) mimic sanity in superlative fashion but also moral rebirth, salvation, and absolute reform, or perhaps transformation into a super-citizen" (1976, p. 434). Or Millon (1996, pp. 445–446) "Unconstrained by honesty and truth, they (antisocial types)

of the signature characteristics of the modern psychopath is the ability to read the reactions of their victims or their helpers and to build trust and goodwill only in order to further their exploitation. What Cleckley identified as superficial charm and Hare refers to as impression management call attention to the ability of the psychopath to simulate emotions and feelings that he is not able to experience. The same persons whose innate sensibility is one that lacks empathy with the victim or experiences no remorse or guilt is nonetheless able to perform these emotions—to "mimic" normality in Cleckley's terms—in order to achieve ulterior objectives. The gap between appearance and reality in which the psychopath is able to mask his deep disturbance is paralleled by his extraordinary ability to appear to be moved by emotions that he cannot possibly experience. In place of the clumsy, inarticulate, and unattractive exemplars of the late nineteenth century, contemporary forensic psychology reconceives the psychopath as, if anything, more competent than the ordinary person in controlling the impressions of their audience.

But it is not merely the likelihood of imposture that distinguishes the psychopath from the non-psychopath. Underlying his inevitably insincere moral performance is an even more damning deficiency. The psychopath is someone who does not suffer and cannot suffer for his misdeeds. Remorse, shame, empathy, or guilt all involve some degree of emotional pain either in advance of harmful conduct towards others or as a result of having engaged in harmful conduct. Those who cannot experience these emotions do not suffer for their wrongs—nor do they even suffer as deeply as others for the punishments that may result from these wrongs. Texts on psychopathy remark on the adaptability of persons in this population to the harshness and humiliations of prison life, the low level of anxiety experienced in situations that would cause severe stress to non-psychopaths, and the general ineffectiveness of deterrents that might cause pain and suffering in others.[49] The inability to feel remorse—no matter how adept the performance—is linked to the

---

weave impressive tales of competency and reliability. ... Alert to weaknesses in others they play their games of deception with considerable skill." See also Hare (1999, pp. 46–51), who offers numerous vignettes illustrating the psychopath's skill at impression management and pleasure in duping others.

49   This inability to experience painful emotions is sometimes referred to as shallowness of emotions. For example, Hare writes: "While the cognitions and interpersonal interactions of most members of our species are heavily laden with emotion, the inner life, experiences, and behaviors of psychopaths seem shallow and emotionally barren (1998, p. 105)." On the superior adaptability of those with psychopathic or antisocial personality disorders to prison life, see Cleckley: "Even when under life sentence, the psychopath tends more readily than others to obtain parole and become again a social menace (1976, p. 434)." Regarding the ineffectuality of punishment, Millon observes, "(Rather) than being a deterrent, it may reinforce their rebelliousness and their desire for retribution (Millon, 1996, p. 454)." More generally, Blair et al (2005, p. 48) report on substantial body of research about psychopath's "attenuated experience, not of all emotional states, but specifically anxiety or fear."

psychopath's general immunity from the anguish of emotional pain for the harm he does and from the punishments that might follow.

In the following section, we shall see then that those who have been diagnosed as psychopathic enter the legal domain under a heavy burden not only as someone who is likely to reoffend, who is unresponsive to treatment, and who is psychologically and possibly biologically different from non-psychopaths but also as someone who can perform but not experience or suffer from the moral emotions that are used to demonstrate character. From this vantage point, we can say that contemporary representations offer a set of instructions for reading the emotions of those who have been diagnosed with psychopathy or antisocial personality disorder. The absence of remorse after a grievous crime becomes a symptom of a deep characterological flaw that portends continuing danger. But the enactment or demonstration of remorse is equally problematic. The moral performance of the psychopath is framed in such a way that appearance and reality are reversed—the more convincing the performance to the layperson, the greater the proof that the performer is an accomplished psychopath. How this expert framing of the psychopath's demonstrations of remorse contributes to the death narrative will be considered below.

Mobilizing Moral Indignation—Capital Trials, Psychopathy, and Remorse

Below, my focus is on how the characterization of the offender as remorseless is used to mobilize moral indignation in behalf of a sentence of death. I base my discussion of these narratives on those judgments and appeals of judgments that cite as one of the grounds for the appeal the inclusion or exclusion of evidence regarding remorse during the penalty phase.[50] Where possible, I have also supplemented these texts with other accounts in books and newspapers of the same

---

50   The population of cases for this analysis was generated in the following manner. Using *LexisNexis,* I used the search advisor to identify judgments in capital cases in which remorse or its derivatives were mentioned at least five times in decisions pertaining to the penalty phase. The search instruction that I used was "atleast5(remors!)" and "death penalty". This search was conducted on August 23, 2012. I selected the time period from 1/1/1990 to 12/31/2011and this generated 361 judgments. I chose 1990 as the starting point because it was only by this time that a substantial jurisprudence dealing with remorse in capital punishment had begun to accumulate. The database from which I drew these cases is listed in *LexisNexis* as "Federal and State cases combined." I chose this database because it has the most complete listing of published cases currently available to researchers. Since my concern was to identify how prosecutors characterized death penalty defendants to jurors in terms of the presence or absence of remorse, I selected from my population (of all capital cases between 1/1/1990 and 12/31/2011 in which remorse was mentioned at least five times in judgments pertaining to the penalty phase) only those cases in which portions of the prosecutor's address to the jury regarding the defendant's remorse was excerpted in the judgment. I ended with 190 cases that met these criteria. Since only two of these

events. As mentioned above, I have drawn from but also modified Garfinkel's typology of public denunciation in identifying the different components of this process. At the core of the denunciation is a rite of passage from one status to another—a transitional process in which the person or social object is symbolically reconstituted in such a way as to demote him in the social order—in this case, from someone worthy of life in spite of his grievous crime to someone for whom only death is the appropriate penalty. It is the representation of the remorseless offender that lies at the heart of this transformation and it is towards a deeper understanding of this process that the following analysis is directed.

Reading Silences—Conceiving the Remorseless Offender

As noted above, when it comes to demonstrations of remorse, there is no such thing as a non-performance. Silence, reserve, or impassivity, when judicial and communal expectations demand a visible display of feeling, are construed as signs no less revealing than the most elaborate of self-presentations. Yet, for a variety of reasons, whether strategic, principled, or simply misconceived, some among the convicted choose or are instructed to remain silent or, if willing to speak at all, exercise their right to allocution to deliberately not call attention to their feelings of remorse. In some cases, the evidence available to the prosecution is so damaging to any credible claim of remorse that arguably, the raising of it will only invite a devastating rebuttal. But other cases suggest the deeper dilemmas that confront the capital offender. It is not just that, as others have concluded, those who did not plead guilty in the first place, face insuperable hurdles in now convincing the same jury that they have moved from hope for acquittal to sincere self-condemnation.[51] The gravity and the intensity of the crimes are such that, from the standpoint of moral economy, the offender and their counsel may decide that since no expression is commensurate with the harm wrought by the offense, avoidance of the issue is the best option. Such calculations appear to have figured in at least one instance in which the defendant in consultation with his lawyer decided that since "this was such a grievous, horrible murder, that there is nothing I could put in front of this jury that would make them have enough mercy on me to give me life rather than death … they may feel that because, after being found guilty of this crime, if I come in here and plead for mercy, that may turn them off, and make them want to give me death." As a result, his statement to the jury merely recounted his circumstances:

> Ladies and Gentlemen of the Jury, I stand before you not to plead for my life. I
> feel that's wrong and improper and basically disrespectful to the victim's family

---

190 cases involved a female defendant, I have used "he" as the generic pronoun in this section of the paper.

51   Sundby, "The Capital Jury and Absolution: The Intersection of Trial Strategy, Remorse, and the Death Penalty,"1998, *Cornell L.R.*, pp. 1557–1598.

and to mine. ... The State has pictured me as being a monster, as being a rapist, as being a violent individual., but as you heard from my family, that's not so. The State only presents one side of the picture. There's two sides to every story. And the State just presents the negative side.The jury has found me guilty of these allegations, and now it's the jury's turn to render a verdict. And that verdict is either life in jail or death. That's all I have to say.[52]

Even in cases where the defendant has pleaded guilty, silence may be a plausible strategy in light of the daunting expectations of what might be required.[53] Yet, legal forums, as do other settings for moral performances, operate on the assumption that what is not shown is also not felt. The silence of the defendant then becomes the blank slate on which the prosecutor can map the identity of the remorseless offender.

Indeed, it is this silence that will define the essence of at least some of the offenders for whom capital punishment is sought. In the following excerpt, the prosecutor addresses the jury about a defendant who chose not to testify despite his guilty plea for the crime for which he was convicted: "I was waiting for M. to express remorse, to apologize to somebody for what he had done and what he had taken. ... I did not hear any of that remorse ...."[54]

Later, in the same speech, the prosecutor continues:

Now, at no time did I hear any remorse. Hear a tear. I mean, we have all felt guilty about things in life. It's a human reaction, but granted, we haven't killed people. We are not mass murderers. But there's no feeling of guilt. There is absolutely no feeling of guilt ...[55]

In another case, it is this absence that negates any other claim that the offender might make to show that he is no longer the same person who committed the crime:

But I submit to you that there's one thing that cuts against this man having changed and become a Christian, and that is simply nowhere in this record,

---

52 *Shelton v. State* [1999] 744 A. 2nd 465 (Delaware) at p. 501.

53 In another instance, the defendant had drafted a statement that alludes to other problems in showing remorse: "People say that I don't show any emotion but that is not true. When I think about what happened I do cry and ask forgiveness from the (victims') families when I am in my cell at night or think about what happened. ... I have told them that I am sorry and meant it, when I say these things to them though, someone say's [sic] that I don't mean it or when I don't say anything they say that I don't have any remorse but the people who make these statements have not sat down with me to see what I am feeling ..." Ultimately, on advice of defense counsel, the statement was not read to the jury, *State v. Bey* [1999] Supreme Ct. of New Jersey, 736 A. 2nd 469 at p. 494.

54 *Sims. v. Brown* [2005] U.S. App. (9th Circuit) Lexis 26806, p. 74.

55 ibid p. 75.

nowhere from that witness stand have you heard one person say that this Defendant has shown any remorse or any sorrow over the death of his wife, over what he has done. None.[56]

Or the absence is demonstrated at a crucial moment when the true character of the defendant is revealed:

What did he do at the scene after he's just done this to these two people? Does he say, I feel bad? Does he say, God, what have I done? No. He's worried about himself, as he always is, first and foremost. He tells his brother T., I may go to prison for this if I'm caught....

Does he have a breakdown when his mom asks him, gee, son, what happened, your hands are cut? I got jumped by some Mexicans at McDonald's. He is able to say that with a straight face. Does he seem like he is feeling any remorse at that time, knowing the scene he has just left? Does he make an anonymous call to the authorities, hey, you might want to run out to the residence and take a look, so that maybe they (the victims of the murder) don't have to be discovered by a member of their own family or neighbor. He is content to just let them rot there.[57]

The impact of this absence lies in the contrasts to which the prosecutor calls attention. For one, these revealing moments stand out as the extreme obverse of how a "normal" member of the community would feel in a similar circumstance. Here the connection is explicit:

I listened as the defense witnesses testified yesterday for any evidence or testimony pertaining to the victim. And there was. The defendant's grandmother testified, bless her heart, that she not only prays for (the defendant) but she prays for the victim and the victim's family. What a nice thing. What a human being. What a nice person from a nice family ...

Do you see what I mean? He's not like them. He doesn't share in their goodness, he doesn't share in their compassion, he doesn't share in their humanity.[58]

Or, as expressed in another address to the jury:

I suggest that all human beings have some kind of light in them, some kind of compassion, some kind of remorse. (Defendant) never had the light. It is out. He's not going to feel remorseful today, one year from now or sixty years from now, he's not going to have any remorse.[59]

---

56   *State v. Stephenson* [2005] Tenn. Crim. Appeal, Lexis 208, at p. 59.
57   *People v. Pollock* [2004)] 32 Cal.4th 1153 at p. 1184.
58   *People v. Jurado* [2006] 38 Cal. 4th 72 at p. 141.
59   *State of New Jersey v. Wakefield* [2008])190 N.J. 397 at p. 468.

The gap between what one should feel and what the offender has shown is enough to expel them from the moral community as defined by the presence or absence of feelings of remorse—which in turn incorporates other moral emotions such as empathy and compassion—that members are expected to experience and show in similar circumstances.

But there is another contrast that is equally important to the portrayal of the defendant as apart from the moral community—the gap between his suffering and the suffering he has inflicted. Almost all the crimes for which contemporary courts seek the death penalty involve forms of violence that are grouped under such categories as brutality, heinousness, and the like—categories that by themselves already call into question the defendant's remorsefulness at the time of the murder. The prosecutor can then summon moral indignation by pointing to the imbalance between the harm wrought by the remorseless defendant and the defendant's own lack of mental anguish:

> The life in prison, is he going to spend it brooding and contemplating about the evil he has done? You think he is going to have that knot in his stomach? You think he will think about the lives he has taken? The years he has stolen? Has he yet? Has he come out and said to anyone that tearfully he is sorry for what happened, that he thinks about it every day, that can't sleep at night? That he can't eat? That he feels guilty and he can't take it any longer? Will he spend the rest of his life in remorse or will it be like you hear on the tape: ... me first, satisfy my needs today.[60]

Or, there is the contrast between the suffering that is inflicted and the absence of feeling by the defendant. Here is how a prosecutor compares the impact of what the defendant did and the defendant's reaction:

> This defendant did all that (fired his gun and killed two people) in the presence of an 18-month-old boy, who now fears sirens, fears police, fears ambulances and those are the folks he's supposed to trust and believe in. Will he get over it? Who knows? The thing we do know is he will have to live with it for the rest of his life. We don't know whether he's (the defendant) concerned about it at all folks. We really don't.[61]

The suffering of the innocent and untainted victim stands in stark contrast to the indifference and callousness of the remorseless perpetrator. He is separated from the rest of humanity not so much by his violent deed as by his failure to acknowledge what he has done and his unwillingness to suffer for what he has done.

---

60 *Sims v. Brown* (n 54) p. 75.
61 *Lucero v. State of Texas* [2008] Texas Criminal Appeal 219 at p. 38.

Yet, as Garfinkel has stated, the project of the degradation ceremony is not just to condemn the act and the perpetrator but to render the act and the feelings that accompanied it as the embodiment of who the perpetrator is: "What he is now is what, 'after all' he was all along."[62] The absence of remorse—the callousness and indifference toward the victim that was expressed in this particular crime and at this particular time—must be shown to be devoid of "contingency, accident, or coincidence." The true status passage in the movement from convicted capital offender to deathworthy capital offender is proof that the remorseless, callous, unempathetic individual who performed deadly acts of violence with no feeling for his victim is who he will be for all times and all places.

It is this transformation that is accomplished through the lay and expert invocation of the clinical categories of antisocial personality disorder, psychopathy, and sociopath. Consistent with contemporary clinical representations, the offender is "reconstituted" as someone whose absence of moral emotions is the defining attribute of their pathology—a pathology that had an early onset and is virtually incurable. Let us consider the following excerpt from a precedent—setting case in which the only evidence put to the jury in the penalty phase was that of the psychiatrist. After hearing the witness testify that the offender was a "severe sociopath on the far end of the sociopathic scale," the prosecutor continues:

Q: No conscience, no remorse, no guilt feelings?

A: No. He has none.

Q.:Now, Dr. (G.), what is your prognosis in this case?

A: Oh, he will continue his previous behavior that which he has done in the past. He will do it again in the future.

Q: All right. So, were he released into society, I take it then, you would not expect his behavior to differ from what it has been?

A: If anything it would only get worse.

Q: Now, Dr. G., this sociopathic personality that S. has is this a condition that will improve with time? I guess what I'm asking you, is this: Is this a stage that he is passing through that he will grow out of?

A: No. This is not what you would consider a stage. This is a way of life. Just as you work every day, well his personality comes out in his behavior, but is not a stage he is going through. It's only something he will continue.[63]

---

62   Garfinkel (n 7) p. 422.

63   *Smith v. Estelle* [1979] U.S. Court of Appeal, 602 F. 2nd, 694 (5th Circ.) at p. 697. This is an excerpt from a landmark case that went to the U.S. Supreme Court which vacated the death sentence that was imposed on Benjamin Smith and ordered new hearing in *Estelle, Corrections Director v. Smith,* Supreme Ct. of the U.S., May 1981, 454 U.S. 454. The appeal succeeded on the grounds that Smith's 5th amendment rights against self-incrimination were breached because he was not informed of his right to refuse to be evaluated by the psychiatrist appointed by the prosecutor. The psychiatrist who participated in these proceedings, Dr. James Grigson, became well-known both because

The interview concludes with this exchange:

Q: Now, Dr. G., I believe you have stated that this man has no remorse or sorrow
for what he has done?
A: No. He has none.

Or as one prosecutor expressed it in more colloquial terms after describing the
defendant as having "no remorse for what he did":

this man is especially evil, and this man is especially deserving of the
death penalty. This is not human weakness, ladies and gentlemen. This is
evil. ... this defendant was not forced into evil because of some environmental
factor. This defendant had everything going for him. He chose evil, ladies
and gentlemen ... all you have heard from the defendant are lies, ladies and
gentlemen. He has not changed a bit over the years. He is still the same dangerous
sociopath that he always has been.[64]

The exclusion of environmental causes—the biologizing of the condition—
widens further the distance between the perpetrator and the community as in this
excerpt from a prosecutor's address to the jury:

He shoots C., and there's no remorse. Let's talk about the definition of remorse.
I looked it up in the dictionary: ' A deep torturing sense of guilt felt over a
wrong that one has done.' Which we know sociopaths can't do. He shoots C., no
remorse. Killed A., no remorse. Shoots C. again, it's getting easier. No remorse.[65]

Remorse may be differentiated from empathy, shame, and the admission of
responsibility on the Hare scale or circumscribed on the MMPI, but there is no
indication that jurors or legal advocates work with such fine distinctions. Remorse
is shorthand for a host of feelings that one should have when one does grievous
injury to another, all of which are absent in the remorseless offender. The visceral

---

he had participated in so many capital trials and because of a widely cited article in *Vanity
Fair* by Ron Rosenbaum, "The Executioner's Song: Hanging out with Dr. Death," May,
1990, pp. 140–147; 166–168. But the use of the category of psychopathy to predict future
dangerousness remains admissible as expert testimony despite efforts to exclude it as
"junk science." See *United States v. McIlrath*, Ct. of Appeal, 7th Circuit [2008] p. 50,
for recent endorsement of inventories for measuring psychopathy as having evidentiary
value. Examples of later cases for which Dr. Grigson's testimony serves as a template are
Bronshtein v. Horn [2005] p. 718, and *Howard Ault, Appellant v. State of Florida, Appellee*,
Supreme Ct. of Florida [2010] FLA Lexis 1631, in which state appointed psychologist
describes Ault as faking mental illness, and as someone with "severe psychopathy" who has
"difficulty experiencing remorse." (p. 11).

64   *People v. Zambrano* [2008] 41 Cal. 4th 1082 at pp. 1172–1173.
65   *People v. Boyette* [2002] 29 Cal 4th 381 at pp. 454–455

loathing that remorselessness attracts is then translated into an essentialist portrait of the offender—he is literally made into something apart from the human. Consider the following representations during the penalty phase:

> But, ladies and gentlemen, his act is transparent to the neutral and critical observer such as you are and you all know that no matter what words may be used to try and convince us that this defendant feels remorse and cares for others, et cetera, et cetera, those are words. ... the sadism, premeditation, and ritualistic repetition shown in these crimes are the classic trademark of the psychopath who feels no remorse and has no concern for anyone outside of himself. He's the beast that walks upright. You meet him on the street. He will seem normal, but he roams those streets, parasitic and cold-eyed, stalking his prey behind a veneer of civility.[66]

Indeed, one must beware of his outward appearance of normality and his superior capacity to control impressions. As another prosecutor warns the jury:

> (Defendant) is a very remorseless, cold-blooded individual. ... Remember, appearances can be deceiving, and he's been working on you, watching you come and go, smiling and waving when he's introduced to you. Appearances, ladies and gentlemen, can be very deceiving.[67]

Identifying the capital offender as remorseless forms a crucial part in his reconstitution as a death-worthy subject. If the showing of remorse purports to reveal something deep and fundamental about the character of the defendant, so does its absence. This true mark of character when coupled with its clinical recasting as a sure sign of unalterable pathology invests the absence of moral emotions with the force of nature. Not only is the capital offender expelled from the moral community as someone who cannot conform to the most rudimentary norms of civil society—he is made into something apart from the human, appearances to the contrary. He is the carrier of a deformation that is rooted in his incapacity to feel even though its primary manifestations are in the working of grievous harm on others. His actions are antisocial, his absence of feeling unnatural. It is this absence that makes him unfit for the mercy of the jury and the court. As one prosecutor expressed it to the jury:

> There is something else you can consider to see if the defendant deserves sympathy and that's remorse. Is there any evidence that the defendant has repented or has expressed remorse? I submit, ladies and gentlemen, there has been none, no evidence that he has ever repented, ever expressed remorse for

---

66   *People v. Farnham* [2002] 28 Cal. 4th 107 at p. 199.
67   *People v. Boyette* (n 65) p. 434.

what he did to (the victim) in the desecration of his body, no evidence that he ever admitted the truth of what he did.[68]

Reframing the Moral Emotions

But what about those defendants who do attempt to show remorse or for whom a claim to remorsefulness is made by their counsel? A demonstration of remorse that is credible is enough to interrupt the process of degradation by which the defendant is made deathworthy. The narratives that urge a jury to vote for death do not for a moment concede to the defendant any credit for whatever expressions of remorse are exhibited nor do they convey to the jury that even though the offender is remorseful, he has committed an atrocious and brutal crime for which he must receive the death penalty. The deathworthy defendant must be shown to deserve death not only for what he has done but also for the kind of person he is. The capacity for empathy, shame, and guilt—all subsumed under the signifier of remorse—tend to restore the perpetrator to membership in the moral community in spite of the grievous deed. To complete the denunciation, the defendant's claims to remorse must be countered by rebuttals by which they will be discredited or by reframing whatever evidence is put forward as not what it appears to be.

On the one hand, as discussed in Chapter 2, because of the problematic relationship between appearance and reality in deciding whether or not remorse is genuine, for every narrative that purports to reveal the defendant as incontrovertibly remorseful, there is an equally compelling counter-narrative that can also be crafted from the same pool of evidence. Indeed, the polarization described by one judge in her dissent in a case in which the defendant was sentenced to death can be generalized to other capital cases in the penalty phase:

> There were essentially two narratives about D. that could be culled from the facts. ... The former narrative cast D. as unregenerate; the latter, as capable of redemption. Whether D.'s life would be saved depended in great measure on which of those narratives the jury believed.[69]

For example,, weighing against one defendant who went to the police and confessed to the murder he had committed is a quote from the initial interview in which he is reported to have said about his victim, "we should have just tied her up and taken her life savings and split the country."[70] The later statement is accompanied by the commentary, "again, a selfish concern with his own well-being, never expressing a type a remorse—'I'm sorry I did it, I'm sorry I caused pain.'" Or another defendant's statement to the jury that "I feel a lot of remorse. It was a terrible thing. And if it could be changed, it was within my power, I would

---

68   *People v. Zambrano* (n 64) p. 1174.

69   *State v. DiFrisco* [2002] 174 N.J. 195 at p. 276.

70   *People v. Sakarias* [2000] 22 Cal 4th 596 at p. 645.

change it."[71] is rebutted by an earlier interview just after his arrest in which when asked if he felt remorse, he replied that "yes"—because his plans to travel were interrupted. Or the prosecutor points to a revealing moment in which a witness testifies to a conversation in which the defendant "laughed and thought it was funny" and "thought it was no big deal that he killed three people" to counter an earlier claim to remorse.[72] Or the religious conversion and personal transformation claimed by another defendant is challenged as insincere and manipulative because he refused to give details about his crime, "if he is remorseful, ladies and gentlemen, where are the guns he used to kill his victims?"[73] Or the allocution of another defendant who read a statement to the jury during the penalty phase that he was "sorry I caused so much pain throughout my life to others, especially my family and the families of the victims" is contested for its timing—"R.W. up until the very moment he addressed you last week has done everything to escape responsibility for his crimes? ... That's not acceptance of responsibility. This is a manipulative criminal saying what he knows you want to hear when it's in his interest to say it."[74] If silence allows the state to call attention to the conspicuous absence of feelings that should have been felt and communicated, alleging that remorse has been demonstrated affords the opportunity to discredit the claim through counter-narrative—by recasting what is portrayed as genuine as instead counterfeit or strategic—one identity showing the defendant to be responsive to the moral claims of community pitted against another identity in which he is cast as unregenerate and beyond redemption.

The other approach to discreditation involves reframing what might be taken as expressions or gestures of remorse in persons who are perceived as psychologically normal as having a different meaning when viewed in the context of antisocial personality disorder. Thus, for example, suicide attempts that might otherwise be construed as expressions of mental anguish or suffering consistent with remorse are reinterpreted as "gestures" that are variously "feigned" or designed to "manipulate (their) environment" or "to gain sympathy,"[75] all founded on the premise that someone with antisocial personality disorder would not be able to "feel remorse for (his) crimes and for killing his victim, but would (only) be able to feel remorse for himself." Consider, for example, the following excerpt from the cross-examination of an expert witness by defense counsel after he (the expert witness) had already testified that his client was a "sociopath." In this highly publicized case, the central issue in the appeal concerned whether the defendant's various attempts at suicide were true signs of remorse:

---

71   *People v. Marshal* [1990] 50 Cal 3rd 907 at p. 943.

72   *Cooper v. State* [2003] 856 So. 2nd 969 at p. 978.

73   *State of Washington v. Yates* [2007] 161 Wn.2nd 714 at p. 778.

74   *United States of America, Appellee v. Michael Whitten et al,* [2010] U.S. Ct. of Appeals, 2nd Circuit, 610 F 3rd, 168 at p. 194.

75   *State v. Daniels* [1994] 337 N.C. 243 at p. 289.

And in your opinion, that person (someone who hypothetically has antisocial personality disorder) would not show remorse?

Dr. G. (psychiatrist): Well, it doesn't hold true ironclad to all such individuals, but it is one of the typical characteristics, yes.

Q: And you can't say, can you, Doctor, whether or not R. feels remorse for these crimes?

A: Not precisely, no.

Q: You haven't examined him since July 7th?

A: No, I have not.

Q: So you venture no opinion as to whether or not he is remorseful at this time?

A: No opinion except that I would doubt it very much.[76]

Given the incapacity of the defendant, external signs of remorse must be read in a different way. Here, expert opinion is deployed to instruct the juror to disregard appearances, to understand that behaviors that might otherwise suggest complexity or contradiction conform to the same underlying substrate of a person who is incapable of experiencing remorse. Therefore, the actions of such persons, even if they appear otherwise, are indicative of strategic or insincere expressions of remorse rather than true expressions of what the offender actually feels.

Attaching the incapacity for remorse to antisocial personality disorder also invites consideration of all the other traits associated with the condition. For example, in another cross-examination during another penalty phase trial, once the expert witness had admitted that the defendant had antisocial personality disorder, he was then asked about the other characteristics of such persons, replying that in addition to the fact that "persons with this disorder show little remorse for the consequences of their aggressive acts and blame the victims for being foolish or helpless," the condition includes other characteristics such as "a pervasive pattern of violating the rights of others," "lying, manipulation, and malingering."[77] In another reframing, a defendant who claimed to feel remorse for his crime was described by the expert witness as "incapable of the kind of deep feelings for someone else implied by the word 'remorse.'"[78] by virtue of his antisocial personality disorder. Other capital cases point to strategic decisions by defense teams not to call expert evidence to corroborate a claim of remorse for fear that the expert's finding of antisocial personality disorder will not just negate the claim but place the defendant in the most unfavorable of psychiatric categories.[79]

---

76   *Harris v. Vazquez* [1990] 913 F. 2nd, 606 at p. 613. The legal debate over whether Robert Alton Harris's execution would be televised forms the point of departure for Wendy Lesser's *Pictures at an Execution,* Harvard University Press, 1993.

77   *Bucklew v. Luebbers* [2006] 436 F 3rd 1010 at p. 1014.

78   *State v. Campbell* [2002] 95 Ohio St. 3rd 48 at p. 57.

79   In *Kimbrough v. State of Florida* [2004] Lexis 558, the prosecutor in a case in which the death penalty was imposed defended the strategy of the defense for not calling expert evidence that would have identified the offender as a "psychopathic deviate" suggesting

Among those who have committed grievous wrongs against the community, it is not only those who are silent or who refrain from showing remorse who are the objects of public denunciation. By means of counter-narrative and reframing, the bar is raised to also include those who confess, who profess to feel remorse, even those who claim to have suffered for their wrongs. Remorse plays a critical role in this process because it supplies an instrumentalist justification for the visceral moral outrage directed at those who fail to show any feelings of empathy or inner anguish for the harm they have caused. The failure to feel remorse is not just the infuriating absence in those who do not belong to our moral community and therefore have no "humanity" to demonstrate—it is in addition a symptom of a pathology that marks its bearer as incapable of reformation and therefore a continuing danger to the community. The ritual destruction of the capital offender as a social object demands that he be condemned not only for the brutality of his crime but for the viciousness of his character and the intractability of his pathology. The remorseless offender is rendered deathworthy by proving a correspondence between the irredeemable act and the unredeemability of the person. But the thrust of this analysis is to suggest that the moral performance that results in this degradation is one that is artfully mediated by strategic considerations, the building of competing narratives, and the reframing of common sense reality.

One of the ironies of this process is that, if it achieves its purpose, the jurors will come to divest themselves of the very same qualities of empathy, suffering over the harm wrought on another, and identification with the victim that they found so conspicuously absent in the remorseless offender. The degradation process not only transforms the offender but also those who will decide the offender's fate. The final words that the chief prosecutor addressed to the jury in the penalty phase of McVeigh's trial were about remorse. After describing the stages that juries go though in deciding to vote for the death penalty, he concludes his speech as follows:

> And then there is a third stage that is sort of outside the law that applies as part
> of the punishment process. I can't give it a name. I can't give it a label but this
> is what I refer to when I'm talking about an attitude you might bring. It's that
> emotional stage that most of you will be going through in facing the difficulty of
> making this decision. It will be emotional. I want you to understand that most of

---

that had this diagnosis been available, "he would have gone into the characteristics of psychopathy, would have quoted some of the less favorable descriptions of psychopaths, and would have equated psychopathy to antisocial personality disorder" at p. 14. More recently, appellate courts have continued to evaluate as competent defense strategies that entail pleading guilty or withdrawing BIF (borderline intelligence functioning) defenses in order to prevent the prosecution from using rebuttal evidence that would portray the defendant as a psychopath—see, respectively, *Ault vs. State of Florida* [(2010], 53 So. 3rd, 175 and *U.S. v. Williams* [2010] U.S. District Court for the District of Hawaii, Lexis 79300.

you will feel remorse. It's Okay to feel remorse. I'm sorry to have to ask you to do this (to vote for the death penalty.) I'm sorry you have to do it. But you do.[80]

Ultimately, the remorseless offender who has been reconstituted as no longer belonging in human society is someone towards whom the juror has had to learn to overcome his or her own feelings of remorse in order to vote for death.[81]

Further Reflections on the Moral Economy of Remorse

The murders for which the state recommends the death penalty by and large represent the extremity of individualized violence against others—brutal, multiple, or desecrating or all at once. Those who commit these acts but yet claim to experience remorse present the jury and the larger community with an uncomfortable paradox. How can someone who has committed acts of such grievous harm feel towards their actions the same way as do members of the moral community? The more transgressive the behavior, the more problematic it becomes to even entertain the possibility of a shared sensibility. If the perpetrator of violent crime is like us in how he sees his own actions, are we then as different from him or her as we might wish? The refusal to grant the murderer the moral capital of feelings of remorse is also a reassurance that the boundaries that separate us from the violent act also separate us from the violent person who committed the act. Garfinkel suggests that the moral indignation mobilized by the degradation ceremony generates group solidarity.[82] Yet, in the denunciation of the capital offender as without remorse and as the abnormal, pathological other, this solidarity is as defensive as it is integrative. We unite in moral indignation against those who commit acts of extreme transgression—but we also defend against their proximity to our own inner emotional life by denying them the possibility of shared moral sentiments.

Does this mean that the moral outrage directed against those who have committed acts of grievous harm but who do not show remorse is ingenuous? That, no matter how much the despised transgressor tries to show remorse, rejection and ridicule are the inevitable responses? If we take one recent capital case as illustrative, it would seem that for persons who are placed in this position, the barriers to official and public acceptance as someone capable of remorse might well be insurmountable. Even the willingness to stipulate to the death penalty was not enough to credit Michael Ross as remorseful for the murders he had committed. In this highly publicized case, Ross, who was eventually executed on May 12, 2005,

---

80 1997 *Westlaw* 312609 (D. Colo. trans.), p. 40.

81 For a more psychologically oriented approach to this process of desensitization or moral disengagement, see Craig Haney, "Violence and the Capital Jury: Mechanisms of Moral Disengagement and the Impulse to Condemn to Death," (1997) *Stanford Law Review,* 49, 1447–1486.

82 Garfinkel (n 7) p. 421.

had in 1987 confessed to the rape and murder by strangulation of three young women in Connecticut. Although he had committed five other murders in New York and Rhode Island, to which he eventually confessed, he claimed to have chosen initially to admit only to the crimes committed in Connecticut because at the time it was the only one of the three states that had the death penalty. Even in cases such as this in which the death penalty is a foregone conclusion both because of the aggravating factors and the consent of the defendant, the prosecution would not allow the claim to remorse to go unchallenged, in this instance, portraying Ross as seeking publicity and notoriety through his quest for the death penalty.[83] When he finally was executed, an item in the New York Times quoted the father of one of the victims that "it was just a cowardly exit on his behalf in that he couldn't even face the families."

In response to the question of whether his volunteering for death was "truly out of sympathy for the victims," psychiatrists were quoted as suggesting that instead it was "a grand act of vanity" performed by "a narcissist with a need to appear noble."[84]

The destruction of the violent offender as a moral entity would appear to be as much an imperative of the death penalty as his actual execution.

---

83   *State v. Ross* [2004] 269 Conn. 213 at p. 322.

84   Quotes from W. Yardley. (May 4, 2005), "Execution in Connecticut: Final Day: One View of Killer's execution: 'It was just a cowardly exit.'" *New York Times*, p. 1. Ross's motives were questioned not only by the families of the victims but by members of his own family who sought to have him declared not competent to waive his appeal of his death sentence. For Ross's statement of his reasons for choosing death, see Ross, *Why I Choose Death Rather than Fight for Life,* <http://www.ccadp.org/michaelross-whyichoose.htm> last accessed October 25, 2012. For account of intervention by his family, see Stephen Blank, "Killing Time: The Process of Waiving Appeal: The Michael Ross Death Penalty Cases," 14 (2006) *Journal of Law and Social Policy,* pp. 735–777.

Chapter 4
Defiance

Previous chapters have already established the seriousness with which jurors, judges, and the larger community take the moral performances through which wrongdoers express or fail to express remorse. But no occasion in which remorse is expected more fully reveals what is at stake in these performances than when the person judged guilty does not merely fail to fulfill these expectations but proclaims that their refusal to show remorse is a matter of principle. It is at such moments that the passions that lie at the foundation of community burst into open view as the moral basis for the actions of the court are publicly challenged. Below I wish to consider two such occasions—the first in which the wrongdoer acknowledges that they have committed the act for which they have been found guilty, but counters the demand for remorse with a claim that the act was morally justifiable even if legally wrong. In the second site of contestation, I want to consider those who may well agree that what is legally wrong is also morally wrong but argue instead that the wrong person has been found guilty—and that they are innocent of the wrongs that have been attributed to them.

I approach these sites of conflict primarily as struggles over representation with very real consequences not just for the fate of the defiant wrongdoer, but also for the legitimacy of the court. The formidable challenge that awaits those who claim that their lack of remorse springs not from indifference to the expectations of their community but from other sources such as principled disregard of the law or factual innocence, is not only to bring out the reasons for their resistance but to somehow avoid the negative characterization that is attached to others who fail to show remorse. I emphasize the semiotic, representational dimension of this struggle because it is largely on the basis of benign or adverse characterization that court, community, and other ancillary institutions decide the fate of the wrongdoer. As we observed in the preceding chapter, demotion within the moral hierarchy from someone who has committed a wrong to someone who is no longer viewed as a moral entity can have lethal consequences.

In the first section of this chapter, I dwell on one protracted Canadian case in which the convicted wrongdoer, Robert Latimer, maintained that his decision to end the life of his severely disabled daughter was morally justified, and, accordingly, refused to show remorse at any point in his involvement with the criminal justice system. Defiance as exemplified by the willingness of those who stand convicted to assert the moral correctness of their actions in place of the expected demonstration of remorse is a defining feature of some of the most well-known and politically significant trials in Western history. Such defiance is manifested not just through the articulation of an oppositional discourse, but as formulated by Hochschild, "by refusing to perform the emotional management necessary to feel what, according to the official frame, it would seem fitting to feel."[1] As we have seen, it is through the exhibiting of remorse that the offender upon conviction aligns himself or herself with the state by affirming the rightfulness of its moral condemnation and the punishments that might follow. The defiant offender disrupts this alignment through a stance that is expressed not only discursively but emotively—the refusal to show remorse coupled with a claim that the crime was morally justified calls into question the moral authority of the state to punish the offender for what is purportedly a just act. In the hands of skilled orators and inspired leaders, these moral performances have produced some of the most riveting moments of confrontation between the state and the unremorseful subject not just in legal history but in world history as exemplified in antiquity by the trial of Socrates[2] and, more recently, by the trial of Nelson Mandela.[3] Many of these trials in which the defiant offender challenged the legitimacy of the state were precursors to major shifts in the moral boundaries of community in which acts that had resulted in severe punishment were later redefined as heroic sacrifices.

While the trial of Robert Latimer does not cast so large a shadow, it is exceptional nonetheless. To be sure, his defiant act challenged only a specific policy of the state rather than its political and moral foundation and his performance did not approach the oratorical tour de force of either of the above. Yet, not all persons who oppose the state on moral grounds are accorded even the bare recognition

---

1   Hochschild (Chapter 1, n 4) p. 99.

2   Socrates' remarkable speeches in his trial of 399 BCE were transcribed for posterity in Plato's *Apology*. My quotes are taken from the eBook collection— Plato, *Apology*, trans. Benjamin Jowett, 1892. Socrates was charged with corrupting the youth of Athens and with impiety. After his conviction, he was allowed to recommend an appropriate punishment, as were his accusers. Far from conceding that he should be punished at all, Socrates asked that the jury award him permanent maintenance in the Prytaneum (public hall) of Athens. After the jurors rejected Socrates' recommendation and instead voted in favor of death as proposed by his accusers, Socrates would make a final speech in which he would say to 500 or so jurors assembled that "I had not the boldness or impudence or inclination to address you as you would have liked me to do, weeping and wailing and lamenting, and saying and doing many things which you have been accustomed to hear from others, and which, I maintain are unworthy of me."(Section 38d–38e in Jowett's translation.) The combination of defiance as manifested by the refusal to show remorse together with fearlessness at the prospect of death or punishment can be seen as a total repudiation of the moral community represented by the court.

3   Nelson Mandela's famous statement—"I Am Prepared to Die"—was presented at the opening of the defense in the Rivonia Trial on April 20, 1964. Mandela had been charged with committing acts of sabotage and engaging in criminal conspiracy against the government of South Africa. For account of the trial, see Hilda Bernstein, *The World That Was Ours*, Persephone Books, 2004.

that might enable them to openly voice their defiance[4] and among those given this opportunity, even fewer can communicate their defiance in a way that has either enough moral coherence or contemporary appeal to generate a public following. Fewer still will survive the gauntlet of negative characterizations that discredit opposition to the state as madness, abomination, terrorism, heresy or other like designations that deflect attention from the content of the defiant act to the character of the defendant. The trial of Robert Latimer, as we shall see, constitutes that comparatively rare event in which defiance or the refusal to comply with the expectation to show remorse becomes a primary reference point for the clash between divergent moral communities and the clash between the individual and the state.

But, as we shall see in the second section of this chapter, remorse is also a central site of struggle in the contest between the individual who asserts a claim of innocence—and whose reputation and potential liberty may depend on this claim—and the counterclaim of officials in the criminal justice system that a finding of guilt and the punishment that followed were justified. From the standpoint of the authorities, an assertion of innocence after conviction calls into question the credibility of the entire system of criminal justice. A show of remorse retracts this claim by affirming that the institutions that imposed punishment did so with cause. Here, I have drawn on a number of examples to illustrate the enormous pressures that the state mobilizes against those who advance a claim of innocence to show remorse and the efforts of those who allege wrongful conviction to resist these pressures.

Remorse and the Principled Disregard of the Law: The Trials of Robert Latimer

On October 24, 1993, Robert Latimer, a farmer from Saskatchewan, placed the helpless body of his 12-year-old daughter, Tracy, in his pick-up truck and connected a hose from the exhaust to the cab resulting in her asphyxiation by carbon monoxide poisoning. Tracy had been born severely disabled with cerebral palsy and at age 12 still had the mental capacity of a three-month-old. She was completely dependent on her parents for round-the-clock care. Just prior to the events that would lead to his arrest, Latimer had been told that his daughter would require further operations to correct a hip dislocation that had been aggravated by her advanced scoliosis, a condition that had reached the point where her spine diverged from a perpendicular position by 75 percent. He was advised that the operation would place her in even greater pain than the intense pain she was

---

4   For compelling and somewhat heartbreaking attempt to retrieve a statement that went unrecognized by the law, see Robert A. Ferguson, "Untold Stories of the Law," in Peter Brooks and Paul Gewirtz, eds, *Law's Stories: Narrative and Rhetoric in the Law,* Yale University, 1996, pp. 84–98.

already experiencing. Moreover, because of other anti-convulsive medication that she had to take to control her epileptic seizures, she could not be given painkillers of greater strength than regular Tylenol without the risk of inducing a coma. Latimer would later contend that he was faced with the dilemma of subjecting his daughter to ever more agonizing operations without the ability to limit the intensity of her pain because of the adverse interaction between the drugs she was taking and any pain medication stronger than regular Tylenol. It was under these circumstances, he would claim, that he chose to end her life.

From this brief description can be assembled the primary narratives that would unfold as the prosecution of Robert Latimer for the murder of his daughter proceeded through a complex sequence of trials, appeals, and retrials that began in 1994 and did not achieve a final legal resolution until 2001. For purposes of clarity, I have appended a timeline of the case at the end of the chapter.

Being and Doing in the Trials of Robert Latimer

At the end of Latimer's first conviction in 1994 on charges of second-degree murder, the following exchange occurred after the verdict was announced:

> Court: Mr. Latimer, is there anything you wish to say?
> Latimer: I still feel that what I did was right.
> Court: Anything else?
> Latimer: Well, my wife mentioned that it's not a crime to cut her leg off, not a crime to stick a feeding tube in her stomach, not a crime to let her lay there in pain for another 20 years. I don't think—I don't think you people are being human.
> Court: Is there anything else you'd like to say?
> Latimer: That's about it.
> Court: There's no joy in this for anyone. I know you believe you did the right thing and many people will agree with it; however, the criminal law is unremitting when it comes to the taking of human life for whatever reason. Life was not kind to Tracy but it was a life that was hers to make of what she could. I am left with no option but to order that you be sentenced to imprisonment for life without eligibility for parole until you have served ten years of the sentence.[5]

Latimer's absence of remorse would become a primary site of conflict for the two distinct moral communities that arose in reaction to his crime. I refer to these groups as distinct moral communities because they articulated completely antithetical formulations of Latimer's act as well as conflicting expectations about how Latimer should feel about his act. The first of these communities consisted of those persons who subscribed to Latimer's interpretation of his own actions as articulated in the interviews he conducted with the press even before his trial

---

5   *R. v. Latimer* [1995], Sask. Ct. of Appeal, S.J., No.402 [67].

and as later publicized on his website. Public support for Latimer would be demonstrated in letter-writing campaigns to the Minister of Justice, petitions to Parliament for a retrial, and eventually petitions for clemency after the upholding of his conviction and sentence for second-degree murder by the Supreme Court of Canada in 2001. From Latimer's perspective, ending Tracy's life was a morally necessary act to spare her from excruciating and unrelenting pain. To bolster his claim, Latimer and his lawyer had assembled testimony from medical experts that his daughter was in extreme pain, that the intensity of the pain would increase with another operation, and that there was no medication available to reduce her suffering without endangering her life. Moreover, in anticipation of the objection that Tracy had not consented to have her life terminated, Latimer's lawyer would argue in his summation to the jury that Tracy's condition was such that her parents were making decisions without her consent not just when she was an infant but would by force of circumstance continue to have to make decisions for her as long as they were competent to do so.

But equally important to the defense of Latimer's actions was the defense of his character. During the trial, Latimer's defense lawyer was able to establish that even witnesses who had testified against Latimer perceived him as a "loving, compassionate father." In an interview held just after the trial, Latimer's wife, Laura, described her husband in the following terms: "We're farmers. I know I married the right person. It's awful to go to bed at night when he's not there. I know what a loving dad he was to Tracy ... Bob's integrity is so basic to his personality. He's 100 percent honest."[6] To his supporters, to his neighbors and friends, and to his family, Latimer's absence of remorse was an affirmation that he had acted out of compassion for his daughter's suffering and for no other reason. As one of his advocates expressed it, "(he) feels no remorse because he believes it was his moral duty to save his daughter from a life of unbearable pain."[7] For those who agreed with Latimer's position that death is preferable to a life of unremitting pain, his lack of remorse carried none of the negative connotations usually associated with remorselessness such as absence of empathy or caring or indifference to suffering. Indeed, from this vantage point, it was because he cared so much for his daughter that he had ended her life even at the risk of his own incarceration.

In almost perfect counterpoint to Latimer's supporters were those who belonged to the Coalition—a group consisting of six organizations that advocated for the rights of the disabled. From their standpoint, Tracy's life was not ended because she was suffering—she was murdered because she was disabled. In the newsletters published by one of these six organizations—that of the Council of Canadians with Disabilities (CCD), entitled "Latimer Watch"—Latimer's act to end the life of his daughter was described as one of arrogance at best and cold indifference at

---

6 D'Arcy Jenish, "What Would You Do?" *Maclean's Magazine*, November 28, 1994, p. 22.

7 Arthur Schafer, *Winnipeg Free Press*, "Justice denied: Latimer case exposes flaws in legal system," December 7, 2007, p. A13.

worst.[8] Granted the status of intervenors in the appeal of conviction and sentence in Latimer's second trial, they argued in their factum to the Saskatchewan Court of Appeal that no one has the right to unilaterally choose to end the life of another person and that the public sympathy shown to Latimer—even the use of the phrase "mercy killing"—placed all persons with disabilities at the risk of other unilateral decisions to end their lives.[9] It was the belief of members of this group that had Tracy been able bodied, the argument that her life had to be ended to spare her further pain would never have even been advanced. Indeed, in the same factum, the Coalition quoted from Laura Latimer's own journal entries, in her communications with the Development Centre where Tracy was treated, to describe Tracy apart from her disability, for example, that "Tracy was extra cheerful when she got home," or that "Tracy is going to be a princess at Halloween."[10] The purpose of selecting these depictions was to portray Tracy as someone who experienced the gamut of normal human emotions and whose humanity could not be subsumed under her affliction. In the public statements and writings put forward by members of this group, Latimer's decision to end Tracy's life was not just a premeditated murder, it was the murder of a helpless child by someone in a position of trust and hence even more heinous than other premeditated murders.[11] As one supporter of the Coalition wrote in an editorial to the Winnipeg Free Press, "Robert Latimer is a remorseless murderer. He has never expressed remorse, or even regret for the murder of his daughter."[12]

In the narrative put forward by the coalition, Latimer's lack of remorse was associated with the most adverse of characterizations in which he was claiming

---

8   As one contributor to the CCD Latimer Watch put it, after Latimer's first conviction for second-degree murder, "The only person he put of misery was himself." See Tom Braid, "The Misery Latimer Ended Was His Own," in *CCD Latimer Watch*, p. 2. For issues of CCD Latimer Watch, see Latimer Archives at <http://www.ccdonline.ca/en/humanrights/endoflife/latimer/archives> accessed on December 27, 2012.

9   As phrased in the victim, the CCD argued that a "mercy killing" exemption in the sentencing provisions of the Criminal Code would result in the following: "If their (persons with disabilities) situation became such that (in the eyes of the their caregiver) death were preferable to life, the could be killed and the care-givers would not suffer the consequences." See paragraph 65 in *Her Majesty the Queen and Robert W. Latimer and CCD–Factum of the Intervenors,* hereafter cited as *Latimer Case Factum–1997.* For full text, see <http://www.ccdonline.ca/en/humanrights/endoflife/latimer/factum97> last accessed on December 28, 2012.

10   ibid [6]; entries for March 31, 1993 and October 29, 1992 respectively. Note that the items refer to entries made in the year just prior to Tracy Latimer's death.

11   For an argument in support of automatically enhancing "mercy killings" from second-degree to first-degree murder in light of public reaction to the Latimer trial, see Archibald Kaiser, "Latimer: Something Ominous is Happening in the World of Disabled People," 39 *Osgoode Hall Law Journal,* 2001, pp. 555–588; see especially pages 582–584.

12   Brian Cole, "Latimer leniency wrong message," *Winnipeg Free Press,* December 2, 1997, p. A13.

a right to murder a child who trusted him, and in which the claim of compassion was perceived as merely a ploy to divert attention from his devaluation of the worth of his daughter. The gap in interpretation between the pro-Latimer and anti-Latimer forces could not be more extreme between the one pole in which Latimer's absence of remorse was attributed to his overwhelming identification with the suffering of his daughter and the other pole, in which the same lack of remorse was attributed to his incapacity or unwillingness to appreciate her as more than the burden imposed by her disability.

Coinciding with the interpretations of neither of these moral communities was law's representation of Latimer and his decision to end the life of his daughter. That Latimer's act was contrary to the law was common ground for his advocates and his opponents as well as a shared point of departure for the prosecution and defense in both of his trials. What was at issue for the court was whether it would recognize the special circumstances under which Latimer had committed his criminal act and, if so, what impact this recognition would have on the verdict and sentence.

But putting the context of Latimer's actions into legal discourse would prove elusive throughout Latimer's judicial odyssey. Criminalizing Latimer's act should have posed no problem at all—that he committed the act, that he deliberated the act, that he knew that his act would result in the death of his daughter were all that was required to establish the death as a criminal act. So obviously did Latimer's act conform to this simple schema that legal scholars as well as public commentators would often remark that if context and motive were removed, Latimer could be placed in the same category as the most predatory and unredeemed murderers in recent Canadian history.[13] But few contemporary crimes are more awkwardly fitted into the available legal categories than are those designated by the popular press as "mercy killings," in which the perpetrator is believed to have acted out of compassion. In a series of comparable and concurrent cases in which parents, medical personnel, or other primary caregivers were charged with either ending or attempting to end the lives of persons who experienced extreme pain with no prospect of relief, the accused person was offered the opportunity to plead guilty to the lesser charge of manslaughter which unlike the charges of first- or second-degree murder, carried no mandatory minimum. Moreover, in the vast majority of these cases, the offending parties who accepted the plea of guilty to manslaughter were given sentences that required no period of incarceration.[14] What distinguished Latimer's encounter with the courts from virtually all of these cases was that he was

---

13   See, for example, Kent Roach, "Crime and Punishment in the Latimer Case," 64 *Sask. Law Review*, 2001, pp. 469–490. Roach suggests that the element of planning and deliberation was so evident that the jury in the first trial had to engage in jury nullification not to convict Latimer of first-degree murder. See p. 471.

14   See Jocelyn Downie, *Dying Justice: A Case for Decriminalizing Euthanasia and Assisted Suicide in Canada,* Toronto, University of Toronto Press, 2004, pp. 40 *et passim* for listing of these cases.

never offered the option to plead guilty in return for a lesser charge and, whether from cause or effect that he refused to show remorse for his crime.[15]

If the criminalizing of Latimer's actions was judicially awkward, contextualizing his action within the narrow confines of legal discourse would present even greater linguistic obstacles. No court in either the first or second trial would allow Latimer to put to the jury the only defense through which the context of his actions might have been communicated—the defense of necessity. It was in the course of trying to establish this defense that Latimer's lawyer had argued that his client had acted when he did in order to spare his daughter the prospect of more intense suffering, that there were no other options available to reduce her pain, and, most controversially, that relief from extreme suffering even through death was preferable to a life of unrelenting pain. In declaring that these arguments did not meet even the minimum threshold of plausibility and therefore that the jury was not allowed to consider them in its deliberations, the criminalized formulation of Latimer's act became the only formulation recognized by the courts. No court would ever concede to Latimer that his illegal act might still be a moral act or that it could have any possible legal or moral justification. As reflected in the quote at the beginning of this section, the court did not have to reply to Latimer's claim that he was right in what he did because his daughter was in so much pain. The only narrative that the court chose to consider was whether any one had the right to take the life of another person. At the end of the trial, Latimer is in the position of refusing to show remorse for a crime for which there was no legal defense.

At the same time, if Latimer's act was criminalized in terms that supported the perspective of the coalition, none of the courts ever accepted the other core assumption of the coalition that Latimer had murdered his daughter because of her disability. Even though the Crown prosecutor in the first trial had tried to characterize Latimer as "foul, callous, cold, calculating and not motivated by anything other than making his own life easier"[16]—as someone whose base character was consistent with the commission of a grave transgression—it is clear in all official pronouncements that referred to Latimer's motives that he was viewed as having committed a crime of compassion. Even one of the appeal court judges who would later decide to uphold the verdict of the trial court nevertheless allowed Latimer to be released on bail while awaiting the outcome of his appeal—a departure from usual practice in convictions for murder. He

---

15   On the important issue of prosecutorial discretion in this case, see Roach (n 13) p. 473 who states simply that a plea bargain was never offered to Latimer and that the case "might have been left in obscurity had the prosecutor offered a plea to manslaughter." But, for a closer look at this process from the standpoint of the prosecution, see Graeme G. Mitchell, "'No Joy in this for Anyone' Reflections on the Exercise of Prosecutorial Discretion," 64 *Sask. Law Review,* 2001, pp. 491–510. Mitchell suggests that the major reason why no plea bargain was offered was because of "Mr. Latimer's strongly held and often stated conviction that killing Tracy was not a criminal act"—see p. 507.

16   Quoted in *R. v. Latimer* [1995] Sask. Ct. of Appeal [60].

justified this departure, in part, by suggesting that "Mr. Latimer's conduct was not motivated by animosity, resentment, or frustration with Tracy. His desire to relieve her from unrelenting pain appears to be the principal motivating factor."[17] If the court succeeded in criminalizing Latimer's act, the degradation in moral status that usually accompanies such convictions was never carried to the point at which Latimer was discredited as a member of the moral community.

Others among the judges who were involved in the case were prepared to go even further in separating Latimer the person from the act for which he was convicted. In the course of arguing that the prescribed minimum sentence of life imprisonment without parole for at least 10 years constituted "cruel and unusual punishment," one of the judges dissenting from the other two opinions issued by the Court of Appeal cited Latimer's good character as one of the primary grounds for distinguishing his crime from other murders. Here, Latimer is described as "a typical, salt-of-the-earth ... farmer ... a loving, caring, nurturing person who actively participated in the daily care of the children and in particular the caring and nurturing of Tracy."[18] If the act for which Latimer was convicted was a crime that had no defense, Latimer was still not to be defined by his actions: "The actor himself was not a murderous thug, devoid of conscience, whose life has been one of violence, greed, contempt for the law and total disrespect for human beings."[19] Instead, his act was motivated by "love, mercy, and compassion"—motives that might well be viewed as virtuous in other circumstances. Indeed, so laudatory was the opinion that the only fault that could be attributed to Latimer for ending Tracy's life was that he had " a severe preoccupation or an obsession with (his daughter's) pain."[20] In a later judgment, this time by the trial court judge in Latimer's second trial, also rejecting the minimum sentence for second-degree murder as "cruel and unusual punishment," Latimer's act would be described as "that rare act of homicide that was committed for caring and altruistic reasons."[21] In both judgments, the latter overturned by the Court of Appeal in 1998, there is a complete disjunction between act and person, despite Latimer's lack of remorse for his crime.

While neither judgment succeeded in reducing Latimer's sentence and while the majority opinion was that Latimer's motives—however altruistic—could not be used to rescue him from a life sentence, both judgments demonstrate the paradox that Latimer presented when his last appeal was overturned by the Supreme Court and the earlier conviction for second-degree murder upheld. Officially, Latimer stood convicted of a crime that if motive and context were ignored met all the requirements for murder in the first degree. Moreover, he had consistently defied the court not only by refusing to show remorse, but also by insisting that his actions were morally justified. On the other hand, unlike

---

17 *R. v. Latimer* [1994] Sask. Ct. of Appeal [6].

18 *R. v. Latimer* [1995] [101].

19 ibid [121].

20 ibid [115].

21 *R. v. Latimer* [1997] Sask. Ct. of Queen's Bench [62].

the wrongfully convicted whom we will encounter later in this chapter, he had suffered no moral condemnation by the court and he had mobilized substantial if not universal support for his actions.[22] The implicit challenge posed by Latimer was this—if someone who commits a criminal act suffers no degradation of their standing in the community despite their lack of remorse, is this an act for which one should feel remorse? And if it's not an act for which one need feel remorse, is this an act for which one should be punished?

What was implicit in the judgments of the court would become explicit when the National Parole Board of Canada rendered its decision in reply to Latimer's request for day parole after he had served seven years of his life sentence. It is the process by which this decision was reached, the terms in which it was formulated, the public reaction to this decision, and its impact on the two moral communities described above that adds a new dimension to our understanding of the role of remorse. Not to show remorse for a crime for which one has been convicted is to reject the moral foundation of the law at what is purportedly the deepest expression of one's true feelings. That this act of rejection might be supported by a significant portion of the community is a test of the authority of the state. Unlike the persons discussed in the last chapter whose absence of remorse resulted in their expulsion from the category of those to whom we have moral obligations, those who demonstrate defiance and who win the allegiance of the public cannot be so easily disregarded. The encounter between Latimer and the parole board—to be considered in the next section—and its outcome, testifies to just how much pressure the state is willing to exert to align the feelings of the offender with the expectations of the court and how tenacious a defiant wrongdoer must be to resist this pressure.

The National Parole Board and the Limits of Law

During Latimer's parole board hearing on December 5, 2007, the following exchange occurred between Latimer and a member of the board:

> Member: You don't feel you're guilty?
> Latimer: It was the right thing to do. The law feels I need to be punished. We need law and that. But if the law allows mutilation of a child then someone needs to alter that thinking.[23]

---

22   For example, included even in the 2001 judgment of the Supreme Court of Canada that resulted in Latimer's incarceration for second-degree murder was the following statement— "... we are mindful of Mr. Latimer's good character and standing in the community, his tortured anxiety about Tracy's well-being and his laudable perseverance as a caring and involved parent." *R. v. Latimer* [2001] SCC [85]. As Joane Martel has expressed it: "What was rather exceptional about Latimer, though, was the criminal justice's inability to pigeonhole him in an 'unsympathetic' category of offenders." See Joane Martel, "Remorse and the Production of Truth," 12 (4) *Punishment and Society* (2010), pp. 414–437 at p. 429.

23   See Gary Bauslaugh, *Robert Latimer,* James Lorimer, Toronto, 2010, p. 78.

Later in the same hearing, another of the three board members had this exchange with Latimer:

> Member: You said you would do it all over again ... you have expressed some views of the law I find to be interesting ... there are all sorts of people who hold moral views that say we'd all be better off if we could go and kill a lot of people ... we don't see it that way ... why are you different?
> Latimer: That I want to kill a lot of people?
> Member: Why do you have the moral authority to take someone else's life?
> Latimer: I can only go by what I'd want in my own circumstances ... the laws become insignificant when there's something more important ... the laws were less important than Tracy was.[24]

For those who resist the demand to show remorse for the crimes for which they have been convicted, the pressure exerted by the state through its jurisdiction over parole can be far greater after conviction than before. This is because so many crucial decisions still remain to be made about when and to what degree the incarcerated individual will regain their freedom. But for persons such as Latimer who are serving life sentences, the power of the parole board over their release from incarceration is at its most sweeping. Under Canadian law, a life sentence is a sentence that must be served for the rest of one's life under conditions set by the parole board. Despite its far lower visibility than the court, in cases involving principled resistance to the law, it is the parole board that is the primary site of conflict between the state and the defiantly unremorseful offender.

For present purposes, however, what is equally as important as the impact of this quasi-judicial body is how decisions about parole are made. Although parole boards and courts serve different purposes in the Canadian criminal justice system, it is more accurate to describe the two institutions as interdependent than as separate. The narrative possibilities that remain open to the accused at trial are truncated after conviction. Before conviction, Latimer was able to put forward the claim that the ending of his daughter's life was a morally justifiable act occasioned by the exigencies of circumstances beyond his control. However, after conviction and in his appearance before the parole board, this narrative option is no longer permissible. That there could be any moral content to his act or that his act could be conceived as anything other than a criminal wrong for which there is no defense is no longer arguable because as a point of law these matters have already been resolved at trial.

It is in this larger context that we can better appreciate why remorse becomes the pressure point in the conflict between the state and the defiant offender. From the standpoint of the state as embodied by the parole board, and as reflected in the excerpt above, the defiant offender who refuses to show remorse for their crime poses the risk that they will recommit the crime that they feel is morally justified

---

24   ibid p. 79.

and for which they feel no remorse. But from the standpoint of the defiant offender, to show remorse is to acquiesce to a version of their crime that negates its moral content, as well as to shift allegiances from a moral community that views the act as justifiable to a moral community for whom the act cannot be justified. For the unremorseful offender, the price of continued defiance is the risk of continued loss of liberty. The cost of compliance, however, is the repudiation of one's declared moral allegiances as well as the betrayal of the moral community that supported those allegiances.

When Latimer was asked at his parole board hearing how he felt about his crime, he replied once again, "I still don't feel guilty because I feel it was the best thing to do."[25] When asked what he planned to do when and if he were released, he expressed an interest in working to change the law so that ending someone's life because of extreme physical suffering would no longer be a crime. The parole board rejected his request and the reasons provided in the decision reveal the unbridgeable gap between the demonstration of remorse that the board wanted and the orientation towards his crime that Latimer actually exhibited. From the vantage point of the board, taking responsibility meant accepting the "real" reasons why he rejected medical intervention in place of the reasons he gave: "You denied any connection between your personal phobias for blood and infections and your difficulties coping with the medical care required by your daughter." Not to acknowledge these reasons opened Latimer to the charge that "(his) replies externalized responsibility."[26] Accepting responsibility meant recognizing that his problems were the cause of his refusal to allow his daughter to have the operation, and not the external dangers to which he referred.

Equally at odds with the expectations of the board was Latimer's lack of self-condemnation and lack of suffering for what he had done apart from the deprivations he had endured as a result of his conviction. His contention that his actions were "merciful rather than criminal" was viewed as a risk factor that would have to be corrected by "further intervention."[27] But perhaps there is no better illustration of the gap between parole board as upholder of the law and the defiant offender than the discussion about how Latimer felt when he took his daughter's life. In a series of exchanges, one of the board members had characterized his act "as a very cold way to do this, to take your daughter and place her in the car and then wait for her to die" and had further interjected that his act was "premeditated ... and that (he) was not overwhelmed with grief at the moment." Latimer had replied that, "... it was a very personal thing ... It wasn't like a big guilt trip. I still don't feel guilty. I still feel it was the best thing to do ... what I was thinking was that this was the best thing for her. It wasn't, as you characterized

---

25   As quote in "Latimer denied early prison release for killing daughter," *Ottawa Citizen,* December 6, 2007.

26   NPB (National Parole Board) Pre-Release Decision Sheet, December 5, 2007, p. 5.

27   ibid p. 4.

it, cold."[28] In refusing Latimer's application, the parole board wrote: "You seem unwilling to examine your behavior or circumstances at the time of the offence and take the position your actions were not wrong."[29] But this was precisely the point at issue—because Latimer believed that what he was doing was the correct course of action, he indicated that he did not feel remorse at the time of the event or upon reflection.

That Latimer was not only unprepared to renounce his views but planned to campaign for a change in the law, was additional proof of his unwillingness to renounce his criminal misconduct or to undergo the transformation that the parole board required before they could trust him not to reoffend—indeed his "preoccupation with legal issues" was identified as another source of concern about his ability to comply with the conditions of day parole should it be allowed. In refusing to grant Latimer day parole, the National Parole Board would deny him a request that they routinely allowed for the vast majority of offenders with life sentences—86 percent of all applicants with convictions for first- or second-degree murder, between 2007 and 2008, were granted day parole.[30] This request would be denied despite other evidence presented at the hearing that Latimer had "incurred no institutional charges" during his imprisonment and that he had the support of his behavioral team and a psychologist's report, both of which concluded that he would be a low risk to reoffend.[31] The official response to Latimer's request suggested that a defiant and unremorseful attitude would outweigh all other considerations in deliberations over parole.

But unlike most decisions of the parole board, public interest in Latimer's case was far too great for it to remain unnoticed. While public commentary was virtually unanimous in attributing the decision to Latimer's lack of remorse, the reactions of the different groups were shaped by their previously established moral boundaries. For members of the coalition, the judgment of the parole board was a long awaited affirmation of their belief that Latimer's absence of remorse had not been adequately condemned. As one disability advocate commented in praise of the decision "what we saw was such a profound lack of remorse for his action (that) it was deeply disturbing."[32] In an editorial also supporting the denial of day parole, another writer described Latimer in more impassioned language: "No

---

28   Bauslaugh (n 23) p. 79.

29   NPB (n 26) p. 4.

30   See *Parole Board of Canada—Performance Monitoring Report, 2007–2008* at Table 62 at <http://www.pbc-clcc.gc.ca/rprts/pmr/pmr_2007_2008/5-2-eng.shtml> last accessed on December 30, 2012.

31   An equally unusual feature of the case was the willingness of the Parole Board to override the recommendation of Corrections Canada that Latimer be granted day parole. See Ivan Zinger, "Conditional Human Rights and Canada," (2012), Vol. 54, no. 1, *Canadian Journal of Criminology and Criminal Justice,* pp. 117–135.

32   Justine Hunter, "Latimer: 'I still don't feel guilty,'" *Globe and Mail*, December 6, 2007, p. A10.

guilt. No remorse. Not even a glimmer of understanding that Tracy might have wanted to live. Not a hint that people with disabilities can and do value life, that lives worth living take many forms."[33] For those who had defined Latimer's act as a crime against the disabled, the demand that Latimer show remorse over Tracy's death became identified with respect for her worth as a human being. As one letter to the editor suggested, "the unrepentant attitude of the perpetrator" reflected "an underlying contempt for people with disabilities."[34]

For those who supported Latimer's position, however, his continued absence of remorse took on none of these negative connotations. Indeed, unlike those whose lack of remorse disqualifies them from membership in the moral community, Latimer's defiance was itself viewed as a moral stance even if in opposition to the law. According to one editorial, "Latimer is no longer being punished for his crime ... He's being punished because he refuses to acknowledge what he did was morally wrong."[35] But to many who wrote about the decision, Latimer's defiance actually enhanced his moral stature. As one writer expressed it in a letter to the editor, "Latimer was honest and did not tell the board what they wanted to hear; therefore, he was not released."[36] Others would refer to his act as a "crime of conscience"[37] and to Latimer himself as a "prisoner of conscience."[38] The same resistance that the coalition condemned as disparagement of the lives of the disabled was praised by Latimer's supporters as his willingness to make sacrifices for his beliefs. Some would even write as parents or as persons who might themselves be in the same situation as Latimer's daughter that "we hope that we would have the strength to do for our child what Mr. Latimer did for his, and the Parole Board be damned."[39]

But the prevailing opinion as expressed in editorials by leading Canadian newspapers[40] was that of strongly expressed disagreement with the decision

---

33   Helen Henderson, "Latimer only concerned about ending his own pain," *Toronto Star*, December 7, 2007, p. L4.

34   Geoffrey Reaume, Letter to the Editor, *Globe and Mail*, December 7, 2007, p. A13.

35   Paula Arab, "Latimer victimized for lack of remorse," *Calgary Herald*, December 14, 2007, p. A28.

36   Andrew Sargossy, Letter to the Editor, *Toronto Star*, December 7, 2007, p. L11.

37   Spokesperson for BC Civil Liberties Association is quoted: "'No need' for rehab in Latimer's case," in *Kitchener–Waterloo Record*, January 24, 2008, p. A4.

38   John Lehr, Letter to the editor, *Winnipeg Free Press*, December 7, 2007, p. A12.

39   Bryson Brown, Linda Bruce-Brown, Letter to the Editor, *Globe and Mail*, December 7, 2007, p. A13.

40   See for example the following editorials—"A terrible decision on Robert Latimer," Editorial, *Globe and Mail*, December 6, 2007, p. A22; "Latimer Deserved Parole," *Toronto Star*, Editorial, December 6, 2007, AAO6; "Parole Latimer," *Montreal Gazette*, December 7, 2007, A18; "Harsh Decision in Latimer Parole," *Edmonton Journal*, December 6, 2007, p. A18. I could find only one editorial in favor of the decision: "A Justifiable Decision—Lack of Remorse Sufficient to Deny Parole for Latimer," *Calgary Herald*, December 7, 2007, p. A 26.

without condoning Latimer's act. Some editorials such as the one published by the *Globe and Mail*, one of Canada's two national papers, one day after the hearing would propose a solution that closely corresponded to the action later taken by the National Parole Board. The piece began with the ominous prediction that, "if the National Parole Board's logic is correct, Robert Latimer will probably have to be kept behind bars forever."[41] Later the same editorial advanced the argument that:

> ... The Parole Board's logic is not correct. The board is supposed to grant Mr. Latimer day parole if it believes he is safe for release. That is what the Corrections and Conditional Release Act says. It says society's safety is paramount in the decision. In no way does Mr. Latimer's refusal to accept the error of a decision he made in the heartbreaking circumstances of his life make him dangerous.

What the editorial was suggesting and what appears to have been followed in the decision taken by the Appeal Division of the Parole Board on February 27, 2008 in its reversal[42] of the parole board decision of December 5, 2007, was to decouple remorse from dangerousness—to treat remorse or its absence as entirely irrelevant to the question of whether Latimer posed a threat to the community or was likely to reoffend.[43]

On the one hand, the Appeal Division pointedly rejected the assertion of the earlier ruling, that Latimer lacked "insight" into his crime—"your responses to the hearing reveal that you did in fact demonstrate insight and were able to explain why *you decided to end the life of your daughter* after thirteen years of caring for her."[44] [my emphasis] What is significant is not just that Latimer was now credited with insight into his own motives, but that his act was now described as ending the life of his daughter rather than as his decision to "murder his daughter." On the other hand, there is no suggestion that Latimer may have had a moral justification for his act or that the act could have any moral validity as a choice to end extreme suffering even at the cost of life. Latimer was granted day parole because "even if it were reasonable to conclude that you did lack insight regarding your actions and motivations, we find that the Board's determinations in this regard are insufficient

---

41   *Globe and Mail* (n 40) p. A22.

42   Of 441 decisions reviewed by the Appeal Division of the Parole Board in 2006–2007, Latimer's was the only decision to be overturned—see *Parole Board of Canada* website at <http://www.pbc-clcc.gc.ca/rprts/pmr/pmr_2007_2008/5-2-eng.shtml> last accessed on December 31, 2012.

43   The legal argument for challenging the earlier decision was that it was inconsistent with the Supreme Court judgment of 2001 that had explicitly rejected specific deterrence as a rationale for imposing punishment and so imposed punishment for the purpose of denunciation only. Hence, since in the view of the court, there was no need to be concerned about reoffending, there was no reason to investigate whether or not Latimer was remorseful. See "Latimer appeals Parole Board Decision," *Toronto Star,* January 23, 2008—accessed on December 30, 2012.

44   National Parole Board Appeal Division Decision issued on February 27, 2008, p. 4.

to support the Board's conclusion that you present an *undue* risk to society."[45] [original emphasis]. It is still a criminal act rather than a potentially morally defensible act—"in arriving at our decision, it must be emphasized that we recognize the very serious nature of your offence."[46] Moreover, as a condition of parole, he is to "not have responsibility for, or make decisions for, any individuals who are severely disabled."[47]

The Board will neither endorse his claim that there was a moral component to his act nor require that he conform his narrative of the crime to their narrative in order to qualify for day parole. His perception of what he did is treated as irrelevant to the outcome of the appeal. All that matters is that he presents a low risk to reoffend if the conditions of parole are met. In this manner, the decision of the Appeal Division preserves the moral foundation of the law—what is criminal is also without moral justification—while allowing Latimer the benefit of day parole even though he has not demonstrated remorse.[48]

But with the reversal of the original decision, it was now the coalition and their supporters who would challenge the findings of the Appeal Division. The Chair of the Council of Canadians with Disabilities was quoted on the day of the decision as wondering, "if any other killer would be granted parole in the absence of remorse."[49] Another member of the coalition stated in a television interview that "a person who's committed a horrible crime like murder should be contrite and should not be promoting the righteousness of that act."[50] As one editorial stated in sympathy with the coalition, "He (Latimer) not only feels no remorse—he cannot, he says—he also does not acknowledge that he has done anything remotely wrong. The law on so-called mercy killing is clear—it is a homicide like any other murder—but Mr. Latimer believes that he should have been able to flout it and be absolved of the responsibility for so doing. By granting him parole, the Board in effect has accepted that possibility and opened a fearful door."[51]

Principled defiance such as that which was enacted by Latimer demonstrates the inseparability of legal norms and moral performance. It is when these norms become unsettled that the moral emotions that support them are also called into question. Latimer's refusal to show remorse became not just a dispute with several members of the parole board but a challenge to the courts that would impose

---

45   ibid.

46   ibid p. 7.

47   ibid p. 8.

48   In Martel's apt summation, "Hence, risk was used ... as the main auxiliary discourse to shield the moral foundational postulates of criminal law from assault." Martel (n 22) p. 430.

49   Terri Theodore and Tim Cook, "Decision to release Sask. man who killed his disabled daughter prompts anger, joy," *The Canadian Press*, February 27, 2008—retrieved from Factiva November 25, 2011.

50   Transcript of CTV News, February 27, 2008, quoting Jim Derksen from Council of Canadians with Disabilities, retrieved from Factiva, November 25, 2011.

51   Editorial: "A Line Crossed," *Winnipeg Free Press*, February 29, 2008, p. A10.

punishment on someone who acted in defiance of the law. The outrage of the coalition that Latimer could be permitted day parole without any show of remorse, was countered by the outrage of Latimer's many supporters that he might have to show remorse to win his freedom. The declaration whether through the court or the parole board that one is required or not required to feel remorse is then taken as a confirmation or disconfirmation of the claims of one or the other of these communities.

In this case, the parole board was forced to retreat from its demand that Latimer show remorse for his criminal act following a public outcry against its prior decision. As we shall see in the following section, this is a concession that neither the court nor the parole board is prepared to make in the case of the wrongfully convicted.

Declaring Innocence—The Burden of Defiance in Cases of Wrongful Conviction[52]

> His Lordship: Mr. Baltovich, before I pass sentence, is there anything you wish to say?
>
> Mr. Baltovich: Yes, your honour, I would like to say that I had absolutely nothing to do with Liz's disappearance, and I am truly innocent of the crime that I have been convicted, and that is all.
>
> His Lordship: At the trial and today, you have exercised your legal right to stand mute. And let there be no mistake, you are not being penalized for exercising your legal rights, and certainly not being penalized for a plea of not guilty. However, since there is a blanket of denial in those statements, which the jury didn't accept, I can only conclude that what you did was with malice aforethought and with total intent. Therefore, in cold blood, you killed your girlfriend: a young lady that you had dated, someone with whom you had been intimate, a young woman who had, on the evidence, given to you your walking papers.
>
> Instead of accepting the "pink slip" and moving forward, you decided to end her life so that she could never enjoy happiness with anyone ever again. You decided to end her life, to hide the body, and you continued in this decision to cause all this grief and heartache to (the victim's) mother, father, two brothers, and her sister, as well as to members of her extended family.
>
> You do all this with great calmness, very cool, very calculating, no emotion. You do it all as though you were moving figures on a chessboard; totally cool, totally without emotion.

---

52   This section is a substantially revised and updated version of an earlier published article: "Showing Remorse: The Gap Between Expression and Attribution in Cases of Wrongful Conviction," 2004, *Canadian Journal of Criminology and Criminal Justice,* 46 (1): 121–138.

> Having chosen this route and having chosen to stay in this flight pattern, you
> are right to expect justice but you have no claim to mercy.
>
> Your phony schemes of lying to the police, and your schemes to get your
> relatives to participate in the alibi, obviously didn't impress the jury. Your
> actions from day one have been as reprehensible as one can envisage. You have
> high intelligence but you are totally devoid of heart and conscience. [53]

If, in the case of Robert Latimer, the parole board eventually retracted its
demand for remorse, the same cannot be said for the fate of those who profess
innocence unless and if they are later exonerated. A declaration of innocence after
conviction triggers a battle for credibility between the individual and the state in
which remorse becomes a primary site of contestation. At the most immediate
level, a claim of innocence calls into question not only the right of the state to
impose punishment, but the relevance of all subsequent interventions designed
to transform the individual into a law abiding citizen. From the vantage point
of the state, the convicted offender who declares innocence is no different from
the remorseless offender and so attracts the same disabilities that are attached to
others who fall into that despised category. On the other hand, for the person who
declares innocence, even the momentary abandonment of this claim is enough
to cast a lingering doubt as to its validity and thus compromise later attempts at
exoneration should the opportunity arise. The net effect of this clash of purposes
is to create a context in which correctional staff, parole officers and parole boards
intensify their efforts to elicit a show of remorse from the purportedly intransigent
offender while those who wish to advance a claim of innocence must embark on a
strategy of long-term resistance.

However, the contest is decidedly unequal as illustrated in the excerpt above.
In fact, Robert Baltovich's conviction in 1992 for the murder of his girlfriend
was eventually overturned, a new trial was ordered, and the prosecution withdrew
its case against him resulting in a directed verdict of acquittal by the jury in
2008.[54] But I have quoted at length from this orally delivered judgment to identify
recurrent patterns in the encounter between the court and those who declare
innocence after being convicted. First, it is important to note that the person
who claims innocence is attributed all of the most damning characteristics of the
remorseless offender—utter indifference to the suffering of their victim, lack of
accountability for their actions, and no display of feeling in a circumstance where
such feelings are expected from a member of the moral community. Second, no
distinction is made between denying guilt for a crime and feeling indifferently
toward the crime. Hence, in this case, Baltovich, who has denied that he murdered
his girlfriend, is represented as if the murder of his girlfriend is an act towards
which he is morally oblivious. On the other hand, as we shall see, those who claim
innocence must learn to carefully monitor their outward expressions of feeling lest

---

53   *R. v. Baltovich* [1992] 18 W.C.B., (2nd) 215 [25].

54   Kirk Makin, "Baltovich Goes Free," *Globe and Mail,* April 22, 2008, p. 1.

they be misconstrued as remorseful and hence culpable despite their protestations of innocence. The result is a moral performance in which the state interprets as cold-heartedness what may be intended simply as a way of not demonstrating the affect expected by the court if the person were guilty. The gap between the claim of the individual and that of the court could not be more stark—those who deny committing the crime for which they have been convicted assert that there is no correspondence between who they are and the act for which they have been found guilty. The court, to the contrary, asserts that this very same act of disavowal is proof that act and character coincide.

Second, despite the disclaimer of the court that those who exercise their right to trial will not be punished for exercising that right, there is the strong implication that Baltovich's continued claim of innocence will result in a greater punishment than if had just been found guilty—" having chosen to stay in this flight pattern, you are right to expect justice but you have no claim to mercy." Already at sentencing, there is the clear intimation that those who defy the court by rejecting its finding of guilt will suffer not just for their crime but for their defiance. In fact, Baltovich did receive a comparatively harsh sentence for a conviction of second-degree murder in which he was required to serve 17 years before being considered for parole instead of the more usual 10-year minimum before parole eligibility.

Indeed, recently uncovered wrongful convictions in Canada suggest a grim arithmetic in which persons later exonerated nevertheless pleaded guilty to crimes they did not commit in order not to risk the increased penalty that would result from going to trial and then being found guilty.

Perhaps no case more graphically illustrates the cross-pressures that beset persons who claim innocence than that of a woman who entered no defence to a charge of infanticide rather than risk a trial for second-degree murder for the death of her infant son. At the time of sentencing, while she did not defend against the charge brought by the prosecution, neither did she admit responsibility for the offense nor show remorse for it. She did not do so on the ground that she was innocent of the charge. This led the judge to comment at her trial that he was "troubled ... that this case is somehow different than those regular—what I call—regular or usual infanticides where you have a young mother who, because of her pregnancy, kills her baby and is terribly remorseful about it."[55] (Her Majesty the Queen against Sherry Lee-Ann Sherrett, Sentencing Proceeding, February 8, 1999, p. 14.) When the sentence was pronounced at a later hearing, it is clear that the absence of remorse had influenced the court: "Finally, I would say this. Who speaks for Joshua (the infant who died)? Is his life so unimportant that his mother who killed him, without explanation, without apparent remorse, should go free without punishment? What signal does this send to the accused? To the community? Well I speak for him now. He was important. He was a human being. He was only four-months-old. And, Madam, you killed him. In my book, that

---

55   *R. v. Sherrett* [1999] O.J. 5210 [13].

means you go to jail."[56] Hence, it is the defiance of continuing to claim innocence even after not contesting the charge that results in a period of incarceration in contrast to the usual non-custodial sentence for infanticide when remorse is expressed. As with the judgment against Baltovich, the denunciation equates the claim of innocence with indifference towards the death of an infant and hence the tone of moral outrage at what appears to be the mother's unempathetic response. But once again, this reflects the continuing dilemma of how to express innocence without seeming not to care about the alleged victim. Subsequently, 10 years after her conviction, Sherrett-Robinson was acquitted by the Court of Appeal on the basis of new evidence that discredited the coroner's report on which the original conviction was based.[57]

Yet Baltovich and Sherrett may have been exceptional in their willingness to absorb the consequences of a claim of innocence after conviction. Recent exonerations suggest that the possibility of a guilty verdict for a far more serious crime or continued pre-trial detention serve as incentives to admit responsibility for crimes that the accused did not in fact commit. In one Canadian case, for example, the person charged with a crime he now claims not to have committed, also following the discrediting of coroner's evidence, pleaded guilty to aggravated assault and a sentence of six months incarceration in order to avoid a possible conviction for manslaughter and a 6-8 years prison sentence.[58] In the United States, there are similar examples of innocent persons pleading guilty to second-degree murder in order not to have to risk a trial that could result in the death penalty.[59] The impact of the credit for remorse for admitting responsibility for the crime not only increases the severity of punishment for those who are prepared to claim innocence but also provides an inducement for those who are innocent to make false confessions. At sentencing, those who claim innocence are not only susceptible to longer sentences than are those who plead guilty but also to adverse characterizations that define them as outside the moral community.

But just as in the case of those who defy the law on principle, the more important battleground for those who adhere to a claim of innocence is the parole board with its power to shorten or extend the period of incarceration or to withhold

---

56   ibid p. 2.

57   Kirk Makin, "Mother wrongly convicted in infant's death acquitted," *Globe and Mail*, Dec. 8, 2009, p. A11.

58   Kirk Makin, "Case Puts focus on justice system's dirty little secret," *Globe and Mail,* January 14, 2009, p. A7.

59   "Nebraska Bill Would Give Sum to Falsely Imprisoned," *New York Times,* January 25, 2009, p. 25, citing example of two wrongly convicted persons who pleaded guilty to second-degree murder in Nebraska in return for withdrawal of death penalty. For broader perspective on issue, see Daniel Givelber, "Punishing Protestations of Innocence: Denying Responsibility and its Consequences," 37 *American Criminal Law Review,* (2000), pp. 1363–1408. As Givelber points out, failure to accept responsibility can result on average in an increase of 30 percent more jail time in the U.S. under federal sentencing guidelines—see pp. 1373–1375.

or allow privileges through myriad decisions over placements, absences, and contact with others. And the same strictures that applied to Latimer also apply to those who claim innocence. From the vantage point of the parole board, the issue of culpability has already been settled at trial and hence, as we shall see, claims of innocence are treated as products of self-deception or outright fraud. It is in the context of this asymmetrical struggle for credibility that it becomes possible to better understand the pressure put on the wrongfully convicted to show remorse and the tenacity with which these pressures are often resisted. I turn now to a closer consideration of this struggle as illustrated in the published records and accounts of the experiences of those who persist in their claim of innocence and those who were later exonerated while subject to parole.

The Battle for Credibility

The most obvious pressures placed upon those who claim innocence consist of the deprivations that are likely to be far greater for those who persist in denial than for other inmates. A long list can be compiled from among the annals of the wrongly convicted in Canada in which parole was denied or temporary absences refused, or permission to attend the funeral of sibling or parent withheld because of a continued assertion of innocence. Even evidence that would normally favor a positive outcome such as acquiring a skill, being active on committees, or having a record of no institutional violence is not enough to outweigh the negative impact of a denial of guilt just as we saw in the case of Latimer. Equally problematic, those who advance a claim of innocence are likely to be barred from participating in all the programs and interventions intended to reshape the offender from someone who committed a crime to someone who will be safe to be released back into the community. Acceptance of responsibility is the typical prerequisite for the programs that enable an offender to demonstrate to parole boards that they have embarked on a program of self-transformation—a condition that cannot be met without risking the credibility of the claim of innocence. The circumstance of one recently exonerated person convicted of murder and sexual assault of a young child illustrates the dilemma of the wrongly convicted. In this case, the Parole Officer in charge of his file while he was incarcerated is reported as urging him to participate in a Sexual Behavior Clinic: "This placement is considered to be a high priority given the sexual connotations (of his crime)" but remarks that "the offender is protesting his innocence and is reluctant to participate in programs dealing with sexual deviancy."[60] The officer adds further that, "completion of such an assessment is required in order to identify future risk levels especially against children"—implying that participation in such a program would be necessary

---

60   *Court of Appeal for Ontario—Her Majesty the Queen—and W. M-J., Statement of Fact and Law,* September 6, 2007, p. 5. The criminal profile report contains the following characterization: "The subject adamantly denies being guilty of the present offence and as such demonstrates no remorse."

before making any recommendations regarding parole. But at the same time that non-participation in such programs prevents the offender from reaping any of the benefits of parole, it was in part this persistent refusal to admit responsibility that would add credibility to his application for a review of his case years later—as he would later acknowledge: "I flatly refused to take any sexual behaviour courses or clinics—to take one seemed to me to be some form of admission."[61]

The cumulative impact of persistent denial is likely to be substantial. It is no exaggeration to suggest that those who persevere in their claim of innocence are likely to do harder time as reflected in the categorical withholding of all privileges and longer time especially for those who have received a life sentence. Perhaps the longest period of incarceration in modern Canadian history of nearly 31 years behind bars belongs to one such person who refused to admit guilt from the time he was eligible for parole after having served 10 years of his sentence.[62] Subsequently, his conviction was overturned and a new trial ordered after which the Crown withdrew all charges against him.[63] In another of the more well-known Canadian cases of wrongful conviction, a lawyer who had assisted in the defense later informed an inquiry that she herself had urged her client to abandon his plea of innocence in order to be released on parole after experiencing years of deprivation.[64]

But if from the vantage point of correctional staff, the person who claims innocence must be factually wrong, then how does one account for their willingness to suffer for their intransigence—to endure a far more harsh regime of custody than if they came forward and acknowledged responsibility for the crime for which they were convicted? It is at this juncture that the tools of psychology become mobilized to break through the defenses of the recalcitrant inmate. Here the assertion of innocence is approached less as a factual claim to be contested or rejected, than as a symptom that requires therapeutic intervention—in one assessment report, an offender who has maintained his innocence is described as "suffer(ing) from a lack of remorse."[65] For those who favor this perspective, an unwillingness to take responsibility for a crime becomes less a matter of defiance than of denial. An excerpt from the *Royal Commission on the Donald Marshall Jr.*

---

61   ibid p. 14.

62   Kirk Makin, "Man Jailed 29 Years Had Alibi but Police Buried It." *Globe and Mail,* November 8, 2001, p. 1. Romeo Phillion whose requests for parole were consistently turned down uttered one of the more memorable comments in the annals of the wrongly convicted in Canada—"parole is for the guilty, not for the innocent."

63   For subsequent history of the disposition of this case, see website for AIDWYC, Association in "Defense of the Wrongfully Convicted" at <http://aidwyc.org/Exonerations_9. html>. Last visited on December 15, 2012. More recently, Mr. Phillion has initiated a suit for $14,000,000 in compensation for his years in prison—see "Wrongly convicted man seeks $14M for 31 years in prison," *Winnipeg Free Press,* May 4, 2012, p. A17.

64   Drew Fagan, "Lawyer says little done in 'futile' Marshall Case," *Globe and Mail,* January 15, 1988, p. A5.

65   *Court of Appeal for Ontario,* September 6, 2007 (n 60) p. 13.

Prosecution offers a revealing glimpse into how this perspective was manifested during the time that Donald Marshall was wrongly incarcerated for the murder of one of his acquaintances. In the following exchange, the commission is exploring a memo in which a Parole Officer had denied Marshall's request for a temporary absence "as it (was) felt that in light of his unstableness at the present time, he presented too high a security risk."[66]

Q: What was his unstableness?
A: This was period of time when his behaviour in the institution was extremely aggressive towards the staff, towards myself, and towards the other members of the case management team where in one case he threw a chair at one of the staff members.
Q: Are you able to offer any insight into what provoked this aggressiveness?
A: I suspect it had a lot to do with whether he was guilty or innocent of the crime. Although I was not (putting) a lot of pressure on him to admit he was guilty, some people were.
Q: Who would these people have been?
A: Some of the other people—members of the case management team who had contact with him far more frequently that I did on a daily basis.
Q: Was it your sense that his frustration in maintaining his innocence in the face of the response that he was guilty was causing this aggression to a degree?
A: In retrospect, yes. At the time, my belief was that he was coming close to admitting that he was involved in the crime and it was starting to come out.

Given the presumption of guilt that follows a conviction, the gap between appearance and reality in the expression of remorse makes plausible this quest for underlying disturbances that belie the claim of innocence. As discussed earlier, just as overt claims of remorse can be challenged by inconsistencies between words and feelings or feelings and deeds, so also a claim of innocence can be invalidated by purportedly involuntary displays of conscience whether in the form of "aggression" or other displays of emotional turbulence.

A similar search for "abnormal" reactions is also apparent in the therapeutic approach directed at Steven Truscott during his wrongful incarceration for the murder and rape of a 14-year-old classmate. When Truscott failed to break down and admit guilt, even after being administered Sodium Pentothal and several doses of LSD over an extended period of time, the notes of the penitentiary psychiatrist read, "he is so controlled, so pleasant, and so objective that certainly there must be in his subconscious a tremendous control for commanding details."[67] In another log entry, the psychiatrist observes "If he is guilty and is not admitting it then

---

66   Alexander T. Hickman, *Royal Commission on the Donald Marshall Jr. Prosecution*, Vol. I, Findings and Recommendations, Halifax, NS: Queen'st Printer, 1989, p. 110.

67   Jordan Sher, *"Until You Are Dead," Stephen Truscott's Long Ride into History*, Toronto: Knopf, Canada, 2001, p. 376.

this implies that there is a complete repression of the problems involved."[68] As the psychiatrist candidly admitted in his report to prison authorities, everything Truscott said was viewed through the prism of his presumed guilt: "He states that he is not guilty of the offence and that this must be accepted as his statement. The fact that he was found guilty in the traditional courts of Canada is a factor of extreme importance."[69]

Somewhat paradoxically, the assertion of innocence is viewed as no more credible among those who are assessed as demonstrating no affect or an affect consistent with a claim of innocence. In one well-known U.S. case of wrongful conviction, the absence of affect resulted in the psychiatrist diagnosing the defendant as having "a sociopathic personality disorder" because of the "absolute absence of any type of guilt or remorse."[70] In another Canadian case in which the person incarcerated had long asserted his innocence, the psychologist performing the assessment observed that the defendant's "calm, confident, and remorseless exterior was consistent with the reaction of an innocent man."[71] However, he also noted," a similar presentation associated with heinous and egregious behaviour would represent a powerful indicator of psychopathy." It would seem that there is no psychological model of what might constitute a normal reaction to a wrongful conviction.

The available literature, biographies, journalistic narratives, commission reports, and other legal documents make clear that the clash between the state in its unremitting efforts to secure an acknowledgment of wrongdoing from the convicted offender and the resistance offered by those who assert a claim of innocence is part of a daily, ongoing struggle for credibility. The struggle in some instances may involve not just the individual and the state but also those family members or friends who have joined ranks with the offender in support of a claim of innocence. In two of the most well-known Canadian cases of wrongful conviction, the presence of such a support system is itself identified as an impediment to rehabilitation. One of Marshall's Parole Officers included in his appraisal that "there is still the problem of Marshall himself denying his guilt and being supported in this by an overprotective mother."[72] Or in another case of

---

68   ibid p. 395.

69   *Court of Appeal for Ontario—Her Majesty the Queen and Steven Truscott—Appellant's Factum*, Section 696.1, Vol. I, Parts 1 to 3, p. 119 at Para 220, 2001, at <http://aidwyc.org/Document_Library.html>. Last visited on December 15, 2012. Hereafter cited as Truscott–Factum, 2001. Truscott was acquitted by the Ontario Court of Appeal on August 28, 2007—see Natalie Fraser, "Ontario Court of Appeal Acquits Truscott based on 'hypothetical trial'," *Lawyer's Weekly,* September 7, 2007, p. 1.

70   Randall Adams with William Hoffer and Marilyn Mona Hoffer, *Adams v. Texas,* New York: St. Martin's Press, 1991, p. 129.

71   Michael Harris, *The Judas Kiss,* Toronto: McClelland and Stewart, 1996, pp. 397–398.

72   Michael Harris, *Justice Denied, the Law versus Donald Marshall,* Toronto: HarperCollins, 1990, p. 283.

wrongful conviction, one of the caseworkers wrote that, "this writer questions how constructive familial support is. First, if the subject is guilty, familial belief in his innocence provides a firm block to subject admitting or working through inter-psychic aspects of the offence."[73] Meanwhile, the challenge for those who wish to maintain their innocence is not just to resist the inducements of parole but to insure on a daily basis that they do not sabotage their chances at exoneration through statements, displays of affect, or momentary lapses that might communicate an admission of responsibility. Can one express sorrow for the loss experienced by the victim without it being misconstrued as remorse or can the offender attend therapy sessions directed towards sex offenders without this being taken as an admission of guilt are examples of the constant self-scrutiny that must be undertaken to insure that the appearance of innocence is consistent with the claim of innocence.

Under these extreme circumstances, it is perhaps not surprising that after many years even those who were the most resolute in their declarations of innocence might be brought close to the point of false confession.[74] Unlike the experience of Latimer, there are no instances among the wrongfully convicted in Canada in which correctional authorities abandoned their quest for an admission of responsibility. Thus Marshall would acquiesce to a compromise of sorts when he was asked by his Parole Officer to admit that, even if had not committed the murder for which he was convicted, "he was the sort of individual who could have committed a murder."[75] Marshall complied with this condition in hopes of improving his situation just as earlier in his incarceration he had once conceded responsibility for the crime for which he was convicted in order to be transferred to another facility—an admission he quickly retracted. Much the same occurred with Truscott whereby he eventually produced a generalized statement in his application to the parole board in which he neither asserted his innocence nor explicitly claimed responsibility for the crime. Years later, even this isolated incident would have to be explained and accounted for in the application to the Minister of Justice for his case to be reconsidered.[76]

In the battle for credibility between the state and those who have been wrongfully convicted and who assert their innocence, those who strive to maintain their integrity in the face of external pressure—efforts that under other circumstances might well be viewed as virtuous behavior—endure what Erving Goffman some 50 years ago referred to as the "mortification of the self."[77] This is a process by

---

73   Carl Karp and Cecil Rosner, *When Justice Fails: The David Milgaard Story,* Toronto: McClelland and Stewart, 1991, p. 130.

74   For discussion of parallel pressures brought to bear on inmates in the U.S. criminal justice system, see Daniel S. Medwed, "The Innocent Prisoner's Dilemma: Consequences of Failing to Admit Guilt at Parole Hearings," 93 *Iowa Law Review*, 2008, pp. 491–557.

75   Harris (n 72) p. 285.

76   Truscott–Factum 2001, p. 115.

77   Erving Goffman, *Asylums: Essays on the Social Situation of Mental Patients and Other Inmates.* New York: Doubleday Anchor, 1961.

which the self is stripped of its social and psychological supports in order that a new identity might replace the identity that has been lost. The experience of the wrongfully convicted illustrates this process in which the forces of criminal justice are directed towards recasting the truths claimed by those who are innocent as pathology at best and defiance at worst.

Defiance and the Burden of Remorse

Whether in principled repudiation of the norms of the state or as the potential victim of a miscarriage of justice, it is the defiant offender who must bear the burden of expectation for their lack of remorse. Here the heavier hand of the law is revealed as the powers of the court and the parole board are mobilized both to withhold amenities from the stubbornly intransigent inmate and to break down their defenses. But this is a contest that has high stakes for those who carry out the will of the state as well as for the defiant individual. Those who claim innocence may be proven to be more credible than the witnesses or police or legal actors who helped to convict them. Then it may be the actions and assumptions of those who contributed to a wrongful conviction that will be open to question and the burden of expectation shifted from those who were convicted to their accusers and their judges as has occurred in the several major inquiries that have taken place in Canada in the past 20 years. Or the principled wrongdoer who asserts that what may be unlawful is nevertheless morally necessary may yet win the allegiance of the community and then it will be those who imposed punishment instead of those who suffered punishment who will bear the burden of expectation. The next chapter addresses this reversal of expectation.

Timeline—Case of Robert Latimer

October 24, 1993: Wilkie, Saskatchewan, Latimer "places" his 12-year-old severely disabled daughter—Tracy—in cab of pickup truck, piping CO into the cab through a series of connecting pipes and hoses and resulting in her death by asphyxiation.

November 4, 1993: RCMP bring Latimer in for questioning and arrest him on charge of first-degree murder.

November 16, 1994: Latimer found guilty of second-degree murder—Court of Queen's Bench, Saskatchewan—automatic 10-year sentence minimum before parole eligibility.

November 25, 1994: Latimer released on bail while his case is under appeal.

July 18, 1995: Saskatchewan Court of Appeal upholds verdict and sentence in 2–1 split decision. Latimer released on bail while case is appealed to Supreme Court of Canada.

February 6, 1997: Supreme Court of Canada orders new trial on grounds that Crown Counsel interfered with jury through questionnaire administered by RCMP canvassing attitudes towards euthanasia.

November 5, 1997: Second trial of Robert Latimer begins resulting in second conviction for second-degree murder—Court of Queen's Bench.

December 1, 1997: Trial judge grants Latimer a constitutional exemption from mandatory minimum of 10 years, instead sentencing him to a year in jail and one year under house arrest. Decision appealed by both Crown and Defense counsel.

November 23, 1998: Saskatchewan Court of Appeal unanimously affirms conviction but overturns constitutional exemption resulting in reinstatement of 10-year mandatory minimum for second-degree murder.

February 1, 1999: leave to appeal to Supreme Court.

January 18, 2001: Supreme Court dismisses appeals of conviction and sentence thereby affirming conviction and 10-year mandatory minimum for second-degree murder—suggests that only remaining route to reprieve is clemency.

2001–2004: Petitions for clemency launched.

December 5, 2007: Application for day parole rejected by National Parole Board.

February 27, 2008: Reversal of decision of National Parole Board by Appeal Division of National Board thereby allowing Latimer day parole.

Chapter 5

Remorse and Social Transformation: Reflections on the Truth and Reconciliation Commission of South Africa

On May 24, 1999, in Pretoria, in one of the most frequently discussed moments among the hundreds of public hearings conducted by the Truth and Reconciliation Commission (TRC) in South Africa, Colonel Eugene de Kock, made the following statement in reply to a question from his advocate, P.D. Hattingh. With cameras recording and in front of hundreds of persons in attendance and with several of De Kock's victims present in the audience, the following exchange occurred:

> Hattingh: In conclusion Mr De Kock, you have testified before various Amnesty Committees and during your criminal trial you testified in mitigation and you appeared before the TRC and during all these times, you expressed your sentiments about the deeds in which you were involved, the people who you killed, the people who you injured, the people whose property you damaged and so forth, in retrospect how do you feel about it?
>
> De Kock: Chairperson, we wasted the lives of many people, not only those who we then regarded as the enemy, we also wasted the lives of our own people, young National Servicemen of 17 and 18 years of age, we destroyed young men of the same age in the ranks of the ANC and the PAC. There were cases in which people were not handling weapons personally or carrying weapons personally and during such incidents, we destroyed people completely, not only changed their lives, but destroyed their lives. We ruined the lives of their families in a sense, and changed their lives irrevocably. I feel that in all aspects, by living past one another, we destroyed one another for absolutely no purpose ultimately. It was a futile exercise. ... We obtained absolutely nothing as a result thereof. There will always be a yearning and a sorrow which will never disappear and which will never be able to be rectified. That is all.[1]

---

1 TRC Website: Amnesty Hearing, Day 1, Pretoria, May 24, 1999. For this chapter, I have made extensive use of the Official TRC Website at <http://www.justice.gov.za/trc/> last accessed January 8, 2013., which contains transcripts of all amnesty hearings, as well as records of all amnesty decisions. In the footnotes to follow, I will use *TRC Website* as the reference and then give the location and date of the hearing for reference purposes.

Less than three years before, on October 30, 1996, De Kock had been sentenced to two life sentences and 212 years imprisonment for what a Justice of the South African Supreme Court had described as "revolting acts planned and executed in cold blood committed, condoned, and covered up by a system rotten to the core."[2] The offenses for which he had been convicted consisted of assassinations, disappearances, and other acts of violence committed while head of operations at Vlakplaas, a secret police organization the existence of which had been officially denied until 1994.[3] Now, three years later, in a speech that would be endlessly scrutinized, De Kock appeared to be offering a public recantation.

De Kock's words of contrition occurred in the near aftermath of one of the most stunning political reconfigurations of the twentieth century. Until the elections of April, 1994 in which Nelson Mandela was elected president of the new South Africa, black South Africans who constituted over 80 percent of the South African population had been excluded from participation in the political life of their own country. Throughout the twentieth century, beginning with the formation of the Union of South Africa in 1910 by the Boer and English settlers after the Anglo-Boer wars of the late nineteenth century, Africans were virtually denied the right to vote or to hold office in the South African Parliament.[45] This disenfranchisement was followed swiftly with the Native Lands Act passed in 1913 that gave 7.3 percent of the territory of South Africa to the Africans even though they comprised over 80 percent of the population. Racial domination was further entrenched by prohibiting Africans from setting foot on white land unless they were working for whites. By the early twentieth century, these political and economic disabilities had forced Africans to accept the most dangerous jobs in an economy based primarily on the mining of diamonds. Either they worked in segregation as miners in fenced, patrolled barracks for far lower wages than their white counterparts or they faced unemployment. Meanwhile, the combination of political disenfranchisement and close physical surveillance at work prevented Africans from organizing or unionizing to improve their working conditions. Political powerlessness translated into economic powerlessness.

---

2   Jacques Pauw, *Into the Heart of Darkness: Confessions of Apartheid's Assassins,* Jonathan Ball Publishers, Johannesburg, 1997, p. 135.

3   The earliest public disclosure of the existence of Vlakplaas in 1994 in the final report of the Goldstone Commission of 1994 is described in *Truth and Reconciliation Commission of South Africa Report.* Vol. 2, Chapter 7, "Political Violence in the Era of Negotiations and Transition, 1990–1994", Cape Town: The Truth and Reconciliation Commission, *1998.* Eugene De Kock has given a brief account of the commission in *A long night's Damage,* Contra Press, Saxonwold, South Africa, 1998, p. 244–246.

4   I have drawn from the *Truth and Reconciliation Commission of South Africa Report,* Vol. 3, Chapter 1, Appendix "National Chronology" pp. 13–32, Cape Town: The Truth and Reconciliation Commission, 1998, to assist me in my compilation of this brief legal history of apartheid. Hereafter *TRC Report.*

5   I am using the term "African" to refer to the original black inhabitants of South Africa.

When the ruling Conservative Party officially announced the formation of its new policy of apartheid—literally, *apart hood* in Afrikaans—in 1948, it built upon the bedrock of economic, political, and geographic separateness that had already been implemented. What apartheid contributed beyond the already pervasive racialization of South African society was the "decitizenization" of the African population. Through a series of legislative enactments passed between 1949 and 1959, black South Africans were deprived of the rights and entitlements accorded to white South Africans. Beginning with the *Population Registration Act* of 1950 in which every person's race was recorded by the Race Classification Board, additional laws were passed to uphold racial purity by forbidding marriage, adultery, attempted adultery, and even extra-marital sex between white and black South Africans.[6] Other enactments insured economic and geographic separateness such as the *Bantu Building Workers Act* (1951) that made it a criminal offence for a black person to perform any skilled work in urban areas except under black occupation or the *Prevention of Illegal Squatting Act* (1951) that gave the Minister of Native Affairs the power to remove blacks from public or privately owned land and to establish reserves for those who were displaced. Resistance to the economic hardship imposed by these measures was preempted by the *Native Labour Act* (1953), which made strike actions by blacks a criminal offence. Perhaps most notorious of all the apartheid legislation was the *Natives Abolition of Passes and Coordination of Documents Act,* passed in 1952, that contrary to its title forced black South Africans to carry a pass containing detailed identification to be produced whenever required by the South African police in addition to the many other restrictions it placed on the ability of blacks to move freely in their own country.

The primary voice of opposition to these repressive measures was the African National Congress instituted in 1912 and committed to the achievement of equal rights for black South Africans by peaceful means. What ended the non-violent approach taken by the ANC was the Sharpeville massacre of 1960 in which police opened fire on unarmed demonstrators who had been protesting the pass laws, killing 69 persons and giving worldwide attention to the escalating racial conflict within South Africa. After Sharpeville, the ANC embarked on a strategy of controlled or targeted violence in which they would attack government installations as a way of meeting force with force. In turn, the government responded with wide-ranging anti-terrorist legislation that criminalized all forms of political protest against apartheid. It was under this legislative umbrella that thousands of anti-apartheid activists were arrested, detained, and tortured as the state gave the police an ever-freer hand to suppress the growing opposition to its policies.

A final stage in the escalation of state violence occurred under the administration of P.W. Botha whose government proposed what was referred to as the "Total Strategy" to maintain apartheid in the face of what was by now armed opposition from the ANC and its many allies. Launched in 1977 but not implemented until

---

6   The *Prohibition of Mixed Marriages Act,* 1949, and the *Immorality Amendment Act,* 1957, respectively.

1983, the Total Strategy involved using the resources of the state to infiltrate and foment discord within and among anti-apartheid organizations, to develop biological weapons that would target black populations, and to create a secret agency at Vlakplaas whose mandate was to use all means whether legal or extralegal to protect the state. It was this organization that De Kock directed at the end of the 1980s until the ruling party began to reverse its course. By this time, for reasons both internal and external to South African society, the Conservative Party changed leaders and began to negotiate the peaceful transfer of power that resulted in Mandela's election.

In this chapter, I have chosen as my site of inquiry the amnesty hearings that took place between 1996 and 2000, and constituted one of the primary responses of the aforementioned TRC to the devastation wrought by apartheid. It was here that the new South African government used its state power to induce those who committed what were called "human rights violations" during the period of most intense conflict—1960–1994—to come forward and tell the truth about what they had done. Provided that their actions had a political purpose—that their actions were consistent with the avowed purposes of the group to which they belonged— and if their account were truthful, they could qualify for amnesty instead of prosecution under the criminal code. It was a bargain that would prove irresistible for many, especially those who like De Kock had already been convicted and had been given lengthy sentences.

As formulated by its architects, the amnesty provisions of the TRC represented a difficult but necessary compromise between the demand for moral accountability from the perpetrator and the need for victims and their families to know who had harmed them and why they had been harmed. If justice were understood as retribution—the imposition of a punishment in rough correspondence to the harm done—then the amnesty provisions of the TRC represented the giving up of retributive justice for the sake of a full and honest disclosure of the truth. Unlike a court of law, it was argued, in which the more complete the evidence, the greater the risk of prosecution, here the fuller and more truthful the account, the stronger the claim for amnesty. In this way, it was hoped that through the accounts of victims and perpetrators, the history that had been erased under apartheid would be retrieved.

In its initial conception, the amnesty hearings were to be a place where expressions of remorse would neither be expected nor required. In a remarkable decision, especially in light of previous tribunals adjudicating war crimes or other instances of state violence or the legal regimes described in the chapters above, the TRC decided to decouple remorse from amnesty. In numerous commentaries on the amnesty provisions of the Promotion of National Unity and Reconciliation Act— including the writing of the chair of the commission, Bishop Desmond Tutu,[7] but most authoritatively in the final report of the TRC—it was declared after what the authors described as a "controversial feature of the legislation" that expressions of contrition would not be a precondition for amnesty in order to "save the process

---

7   Desmond Tutu, *No Future Without Forgiveness*, London: Rider Books, 1999, p. 48.

from lies and faked apologies."[8] Unlike virtually all other truth commissions and legal regimes in other common law jurisdictions, the TRC sought to eliminate one of the primary sources of ambiguity in the moral performance of remorse. By decoupling remorse from any possible legal benefit, perpetrators, it was thought, would be less likely to pretend to emotions they did not feel and more likely to be genuine about the emotions they did feel.

Yet, despite this resolve to decouple remorse from reward, the seemingly innocuous question of how the perpetrator felt about what they had done became increasingly the moment that most defined the hearing.[9] Whether it was the victim or the chair of the hearing or, as with De Kock, the perpetrator who arranged that his lawyer would ask the question, the response that either affirmed the transgressor's continued belief in the rightfulness of the act or recanted it was the interchange that was written about in the media or shown by the South African Broadcasting Association in its weekly highlights or emphasized in the documentary *Long Night's Journey into Day,* the most widely distributed film on the TRC. Indeed, perhaps the most frequently cited exchange of all the public hearings was that which occurred between Tutu himself and Winnie Madikizela-Mandela, when he implored the ex-wife of the president of South Africa to acknowledge her responsibility for the wrongs that had been laboriously documented and attributed to her and when she responded to his request. The exchange took place after eight days of harrowing testimony, involving allegations of torture, murder, and assault perpetrated by a group of young men. All of the youths had been closely associated with Ms. Madikizela-Mandela and were members of what came to be known as the Mandela United Football Club. Just prior to this encounter, several members who had already been charged and convicted of murder had testified before the Commission that they had acted in accord with her instructions. In a much publicized encounter on December 4, 1997 in an amphitheatre in Johannesburg, with the mother of Stompie Seipei, one of the victims, present in the audience, Bishop Tutu leaned forward and the following exchange took place:

> Bishop Tutu: There are people out there who want to embrace you. I still embrace you because I love you and I love you very deeply. There are many out there who would have wanted to do so if you were able to bring yourself to say something went wrong. Because all these leaders couldn't have been so agitated and say I am sorry. I am sorry for my part in what went wrong and I believe we are incredible people. Many would have rushed out in their eagerness to forgive and to embrace you.

---

8   *TRC Report,* 1998, Vol. 5, Chapter 9 at 39.

9   As Deborah Posel observes of the amnesty hearings, "their public function was to perform the catharsis of the apology, disclosure of wrongdoing, culminating in the recognition of, and apology for, the suffering inflicted." See Deborah Posel, "History as Confession: The Case of the South African Truth and Reconciliation Commission," 20, no.1, *Popular Culture,* 2008, p. 138.

I beg you, I beg you, I beg you please—I have not made any particular finding from what has happened here. I speak as someone who has lived in this community. You are a great person and you don't know how your greatness would be enhanced if you were to say sorry, things went wrong, forgive me. I beg you.

Ms. Madikizela-Mandela: Thank you very much—Save to say thank you very much for your wonderful, wise words and that is the father I have always known in you. I am hoping it is still the same. I will take this opportunity to say ... (to) Stompie's mother, how deeply sorry I am. I have said so to her before a few years back, when the heat was very hot. I am saying it is true, things went horribly wrong. I fully agree with that and for that part of those painful years when things went horribly wrong and we were aware of the fact that there were factors that led to that, for that I am deeply sorry.[10]

The sufficiency or insufficiency of Madikizela-Mandela's response to Bishop Tutu would become a subject of much commentary in the accounts of journalists and writers as well as in the Final Report of the TRC.

In the following three sections, I will take a closer look at these moral performances to show how through approval and disapproval, compliance with or resistance to the expectation of remorse, members negotiated the moral architecture of a newly emergent community. In the first section, building upon the previous chapter, I will describe how the unwillingness to acknowledge "human rights violations" as wrongful actions or defiance of the expectation to show remorse exposed to public view the presence of competing or conflicting moral communities. In the second section, I will return to the aforementioned encounter between the TRC and Eugene de Kock. No occasion better embodied the aspirations of the TRC than the heartfelt remorse of someone who had fought to preserve apartheid and who might promise to make amends for their former transgressions. With this attention, however, came closer public scrutiny. The greater the divide between the former identity of the adversary and the identity they now claimed, the more that was demanded as evidence of the transformation. Using De Kock's recantation as point of reference for this act of conversion from one moral community to another, I will show how remorse became a central site of contestation in the process of self-transformation both as the medium through which the transgressor demonstrated change and as a performance that met or fell short of social expectations. Finally, I will locate the reaction to De Kock's show of remorse as part of a larger debate over who should show remorse, what form remorse should take to support a claim for a shift in moral allegiance and whether certain transgressions exceed the bounds of social reinclusion.

---

10 *TRC Website*—see Special Hearings—Mandela United Football Club, day 9, December 4, 1997 [unpaginated]. See also, Antjie Krog, *Country of My Skull,* New York: Three Rivers Press, 2000, p. 338 for contemporary reaction to this encounter.

Defiance

At the amnesty hearing that took place on March 26, 1998 at Pretoria, the following document was read into the transcript. It is an affidavit that describes the encounter between Mr. Papiyana, whose son was shot to death while driving his taxi, and the person who fired the shot. The perpetrator, Cornelius Rudolph Pyper, was a member of the AWB[11] and he had set out with a few of his confederates to obstruct through whatever means available the first day of elections in the new South Africa, including shooting at black South Africans on their way to exercise their new voting rights. On April 27, 1994, he fired at the driver of a car containing two black South Africans resulting in the death of Viyana Papiyana and severe injuries to Papiyana's brother. Here is Papiyana's account of his meeting with Pyper:

> I could see that Mr. Pyper tried his best to keep his emotions under control. He requested his attorney to let them (Pyper and his wife) see me alone and he did not want the lawyers to be present.
>
> I knew this man was indeed sorry for what he had done and when I offered my hand, he could not grab it quickly enough, with both his hands. Tears were running freely from his face. Before this meeting, I thought I would never have the ability to forgive my son's murderers for what they did.
>
> In my wildest dreams I never thought that this meeting would end with a situation where I was the one comforting my son's murderer and his wife. I still wonder a lot what happened to his wife and children. Mr. Pyper told me what happened that night and he said that he still did not understand why and how he could ever have done such a foolish thing.
>
> When I learnt later in the evidence given by Dr. __ that he was an introvert, a person who does not show his emotions easily, I realized that it must have been very difficult for him and that the remorse was so intense that he could not hide it.[12]

But such a meeting of the minds between wrongdoer and victim would prove exceedingly rare however much encouraged by the commissioners and other officials at the TRC. More frequently, claimants resisted the invitation to show contrition by asserting their continued loyalty to the political community under whose authority they had committed the act.

Occasionally, such exchanges could produce striking moments of confrontation in which the divergent moral communities that still coexisted within post-apartheid

---

11   AWB stands for *Afrikaner We Erstandsbeweging* or Afrikaans Insurgency Movement, a nationalist Afrikaner party that opposed any negotiation with the African National Congress over apartheid.

12   This account is taken from an affidavit submitted by Nelson Papiyana at Cornelius Pyper's amnesty hearing on March 26, 1998—*TRC Website* at <http://www.justice.gov.za/trc/amntrans/pta/lotteri2.htm> accessed on January 15, 2013.

South Africa would be clearly delineated. Thus the response of Janusz Waluz—a member of the South African Defense Forces—when asked by the advocate for the victims how he felt about his role as co-assassin of Chris Hani, an ANC activist who later became secretary of the South African Communist Party:

> Adv. Bizos: What is your present feeling, Mr. Walus, did you achieve anything by murdering Mr. Hani either politically, personally, or for your cause or was it a wasted life? The waste having been caused by you, which of the two do you feel?
> Walus: Mr. Chairman, I can't answer this question because (only) history can show, further history, what happened as also we cannot foresee what could have happened if Mr. Hani would still be alive. ...
> Adv. Bizos: I would have expected you to show some remorse in answer to that question and not leave it for history to possibly justify your act.
> Walus: Mr. Chairman, I would like to ask Mr. Bizos why he expects from me remorse.[13]

Two years later, when Walus along with his co-assassin, Clive Derby-Lewis, were refused amnesty, the spokesperson for the South African Trade Unions would refer to this exchange declaring that Walus's lack of remorse "created the impression that (he) was proud of the murder."[14] At the same time, the Afrikaner Prisoner Association would gather petitions with thousands of signatures and raise funds to protest the decision and to finance an appeal.[15]

Those who had fought against apartheid could be equally defiant in rejecting the moral framework of the TRC, particularly the assertion of legal equivalence between themselves and the defenders of the state. In one highly publicized attack, members of the APLA (Azanian People's Liberation Army) had raided a Bahai Faith Centre and, after separating "black" from "white" worshippers, shot three of the latter and confiscated one of their cars for purposes of escape. In the following exchange, one of the claimants is challenged by the Chairperson of the hearing:

> Chairperson: Are you saying that you were proud and glad to have been told to go and kill people and you wouldn't go to anything that might stop you from doing that?
> Madasi: Judge Wilson, it was a war between the oppressor and the oppressed. ...
> Yes, I am proud. I left home, my parents loved me and I left them behind, volunteered, yes I was proud to fight, to be in the battle, I don't regret having taken part in the APLA. APLA consists of soldiers, different units inside South Africa. I feel that the struggle the African took part in was a good thing; it was

---

13   *TRC Website*—Amnesty Hearing held at Pretoria, August 11, 1997.

14   *TRC Website, SAPA (South African Press Association)*, "Cosatu Says Hani's Killers Showed No Remorse," April 8, 1999.

15   *TRC Website, SAPA*, "Charge Those Implicated in TRC: Says Afrikaner Group," December 2, 1999.

noble. It would take the day to list the number of things the Boers did against the oppressed, the cruel things that they did.[16]

Later in the same hearing, when Madasi is asked how he can support reconciliation if he is unwilling to apologize for the killing of innocent people, he replied: "The platform that we are at today is such that liberation fighters, I will not say perpetrator because that means something else altogether, this platform is such that liberation fighters and victims hold hands and reconcile in this new Africa." For Madasi and for other members of the anti-apartheid forces, neither the means used nor the ends employed to achieve liberation were acts for which one should be expected to show remorse.

But resistance could also be attached to far more complex narratives as exemplified in the much-discussed moral performance of Captain Jeffrey Benzien of the South African police service.[17] By the time of the hearings, Benzien had achieved notoriety as someone prepared to use the most extreme methods of torture to extract information from his captives. In his appearance before the TRC, in July, 1997, he would describe these methods including the techniques that had led to the death of Umkhonto we Sizwe[18] fighter, Ashley Kriel. At one point in the hearing, Benzien was confronted by one of his former victims. Tony Yengeni, later to become a member of the South African Parliament:

I want to understand really why, what happened? I am not talking about now the politics or your family, I am talking about the man behind the wet bag? When you do those things, what happens to you as a human being? What goes through your head, your mind? You know, what effect does that torture activity done to you as a human being?[19]

During this hearing, Benzien had demonstrated the "wet bag" method of torture with a surrogate, showing how he would sit on the back of the suspect and then pull a wet cloth bag over their head, twisting it tightly around their neck thereby

---

16 *TRC Website,* Amnesty Hearing held at East London, April 17, 1998. It is especially significant that Madasi rejects official designation as perpetrator even though he is applying for amnesty under this category. In an earlier hearing, Madasi, who had directed the Heidelberg Tavern massacre in which gunmen had entered a tavern and had shot to death four unarmed civilians had declared: "We do not therefore regret that such operations took place and there is therefore nothing to apologize (sic) because we believe in the justice of our war and the correctness of our struggle." See amnesty hearing into Heidelberg Tavern massacre, Part 7, Cape Town, October 31, 1997.

17 See Krog (n 10) pp. 93–99 for eyewitness account of this hearing. Also, see Claire Moon, *Narrating Political Reconciliation,* Lexington Books, Plymouth England, 2009, pp. 97–98 for discussion of Benzien's confession.

18 Usually translated as "Spear of the Nation," the armed wing of the ANC.

19 *TRC Website*—All quotes taken from transcript of amnesty hearing of Jeffrey Benzien, Cape Town, July 14, 1997.

cutting off their air supply. Replying to Yengeni's challenge, Benzien came back with the following question:

> My application, Mr. Yengeni, please tell me if I am right or wrong, my application of the wet bag method was at the initial arrest, until such times as you had against your will, revealed who your contacts were or where your arms caches were. Could you please answer me that, is it correct? Is it correct Mr Yengeni?

Journalists and other publicists who were in attendance interpreted this exchange as reflecting Benzien's pride in his effectiveness. In defense of his methods, Benzien would claim that they were successful and no more violent than was necessary to achieve their purpose.

Benzien easily conceded that his work was brutal and dehumanizing and that it had exacted a huge psychological toll. Early in his response to Yengenis's query, he had replied

> Mr. Yengeni, not only you have asked me that question. I, Jeff Benzien, have asked myself that question to such an extent that I voluntarily, and it is not easy for me to say this in a full court with a lot of people who do not know me, approached Psychiatrists to have myself evaluated, to find out what type of person am I.
>
> There was a stage when this whole scene was going on, that I thought I was losing my mind. I have subsequently been, and I am now still, under treatment, where I have to take tablets on a regular basis.

Indeed, part of Benzien's claim for amnesty consisted of a psychologist's report corroborating that he had suffered extreme psychological damage because of the clash between the dictates of his conscience and what was demanded by his work and that he had come to feel shame and self-loathing for what he had done. This was offered in part to explain that his selective amnesia over certain details of his operation was not an act of willful evasion but the residue of the trauma inflicted by his work—"I did terrible things, I did terrible things to members of the ANC, but as God as my witness, believe me, I have also suffered." But the claim to victimhood served other purposes as well. For Benzien and for others among the South African defense forces, disclosure of the brutality of their work and the violence wrought on victims was less to substantiate a claim of remorse than to catalogue the extreme sacrifices they had made for their beliefs.[20] For the moral community to which Benzien directed his comments, the very acts that made him

---

20 *TRC Website*—see, for example, amnesty hearing of Major Craig Williamson, Pretoria, September 14–15, 1998 who also justified his involvement in political assassinations as a measure of his dedication to apartheid. Williamson was closely allied with De Kock just before he become involved with Vlakplaas. See Jacques Pauw, *Into the Heart of Darkness–Confessions of Apartheid's Assassins,* Jonathan Ball Publishers, 1997,

an object of contempt to supporters of the ANC cast him as a hero among those who defended the state.[21] So great was his loyalty that he had been willing to risk psychic injury to perform the morally abhorrent acts that were necessary to insure the safety of his fellow white Afrikaners. The amnesty hearings were a site of contestation in which moral communities with antithetical values commingled and the perpetrators' feelings about what they had done became the occasion for defining these differences.

Yet the more frequent approach among those who resisted the expectation to show remorse was to try to reconcile the claims of their political community with the demands of the victim or their advocates. For example, when confronted with the claims of victims whose parents or children had been killed in an attack at the St. James Church in Cape Town, one of the ANC members who had participated responded in this manner:

> I threw a hand grenade; I fired shots obeying the instructions from my commander, that resulted in what we are today talking about. I do regret and please forgive me because it was the situation in South African at that time. ... I know there is no one who has the right to kill. But the situation in South Africa led us as we were young, to do those things because we grew up in a violent country. We were seeing our fellow Africans being shot and killed by whites. All in all, I don't know if you grew up in such circumstances, wouldn't you expect such things to happen ...[22] (July, 1997, Cape Town).

Such accounts expressed sympathy with the losses suffered by the victim while affording a moral justification for the act. In place of self-condemnation or condemnation of the political organization that had planned the act, the perpetrator adopted a posture of regret—the actions were necessary because of the context albeit unfortunate in their consequences.[23] Those who showed regret conveyed that their actions did correspond to how they felt at the time they committed their human rights violation and to how they would feel now if placed in the same circumstances.

pp. 43–44. For discussion of Williamson's presentation before the TRC, see Leigh Payne, *Unsettling Accounts,* Duke University Press, 2008, pp. 91–96.

21   I am indebted to Payne's *Unsettling Accounts* for identifying heroic defiance as one of the confessional modes deployed by "perpetrators" during the amnesty hearings. See especially Chapter 3 entitled "Heroic Confessions."

22   *TRC Website*—Amnesty Hearing, Cape Town, July 9, 1997.

23   Perhaps the most poignant example of this reconciliation between empathy for the victim but loyalty to the party is the exchange over the killing of Amy Biehl, a white American anti-apartheid activist killed during a riot against white South Africans. See *TRC Website,* Cape Town, July 7, 1997, in which one of the persons involved in her death states: "I said that having killed Amy Biehl, I am not happy about that, however, it is such things that have helped South Africa be where it is today." The amnesty hearing involving Biehl was one of the four episodes of the TRC hearings included in *Long Night's Journey into Day.*

If the reaffirmation of one's membership in their moral community were the prevailing response to the request for remorse, this is not to suggest that the commission or the media regarded all such claims as morally equivalent. By the time of the hearings, pro-apartheid police and other state operatives would be asked not only how they felt about what they had done but also to account for their political affiliation. It was not only Benzien who included a psychologist's report[24] in his application for amnesty. In the new South Africa, membership in the pro-apartheid moral community was pathologized and problematized in terms that were not applied to those who had fought against apartheid. No ANC or APLA[25] member was ever asked to justify his or her choice to join the armed struggle against apartheid.

Perhaps it is for this reason that all those whose claim to remorse included the renunciation of their former moral community were drawn from among the supporters for apartheid. When he testified in September, 1996, in mitigation of his sentence, De Kock remarked that "the way people are talking now, it seems like I was the only white man defending apartheid."[26]

But, as we shall see, it was De Kock's own recantation that would be among the most contested of all those who claimed to no longer be the same person that had committed the violent deeds for which they were now seeking amnesty.

The Moral Careers of Eugene de Kock

There have been few instances in the brief history of transitional justice when someone central to the operation of a now discredited system of state violence has come forward both to denounce the leaders they once served and also to give a full account of their own murderous activities.[27] But this is what Eugene de Kock purported to do in the 50 days of testimony that he gave at the amnesty hearings between 1997 and 2000. Perhaps no one among all the claimants who

---

24   For psychological and psychiatric reports on Vlakplaas operatives, see Pauw, p. 91, pp. 204–205. Also, for submission of psychological reports at the Amnesty Board Hearings, see transcript of amnesty hearing held in Cape Town on March 11, 1997— Day I involved in interrogations of Paul Van Vuuren, a police man who was part of the Vlakplaas death squads, Brigadier General Jan (Jack) Kronje, and Captain Jack Hechter, also a member of the death squad. Consider this exchange during hearing: "Adv. Du Plessis: 'Can you say to the Committee, did you have a personal desire to torture people the whole time?' Van Vuuren: 'No I did not have a personal desire to torture people.'"

25   APLA—Azanian People's Liberation Army—allies of ANC in resistance to apartheid.

26   Quoted in Pauw, p. 144; also quoted in *TRC Report,* Chapter 4, p. 167.

27   Albert Speer's memoirs are perhaps a precedent, but even here Gitta Sereny suggests after an exhaustive inquiry that while Speer wrote an eloquent condemnation of the Nazi party, he never quite acknowledged his role in it. See Gitta Sereny, *Albert Speer: His Battle with the Truth,* Albert Knopf: New York, 1995—see especially Chapter XXVI, pp. 702–720.

came before the TRC played a more important role in bringing out the "truth" of what had occurred under apartheid—indeed, the authors of the final report of the TRC credit him with commencing the process that led to the wave of disclosures by members of the security police—a process to which the Commission attributed much of its success in bringing out the truth of apartheid: "The ironic truth is that what brought them (the security police at Vlakplaas) to the Commission was the fullness of the disclosures made by an individual often painted as the arch-villain of the apartheid era, Mr. Eugene de Kock. Whatever his motive, the Commission acknowledges that it was largely he who broke the code of silence."[28]

In the modern iconography of apartheid, whether deserved or not, no figure stands out more prominently as its demonic embodiment than De Kock. As commander of the hit squad unit at Vlakplaas from 1985 to 1993, De Kock and other recruits to the C1[29] unit were given license by the National Party to operate outside and above the law and in total secrecy in their war on the ANC.[30] Operating outside the law meant specifically that both the objectives and the means employed to achieve those objectives were covert since exposure would have implicated the state in extra-legal activity—or activity that exceeded the authority already granted the state in its policing functions. In practice, this meant that not only did unit C1 plan and implement such illegal acts as assassinations, bombings of the homes and meeting places of non-combatants, and methods of torture to extract information, but that all evidence of these activities had to be denied whether through deceit, destruction of potentially incriminating testimony, fabrication, or silence. In turn, these acts of deception frequently required the cooperation of the state and its ancillary institutions such as the courts, police, and those members of the ruling party who had access to this information.

I will give two examples from the hundreds furnished by De Kock, in his testimony before the TRC, both to identify the kinds of actions for which he sought amnesty but also to better illuminate how well-positioned he was to disclose the secret activities of the state. De Kock's disclosures not only brought into public view his own extensive involvement in underground activity, it also provided a new and lasting image of the violence of apartheid.

The first incident involved the killing on December 14, 1989 of three black policemen and their friend all of whom became known as the "Motherwell Four" after a bomb planted in their car was detonated by remote control resulting in all four deaths. The assassination of the three targeted policemen was to prevent them from following through on their threat to expose security police involvement in an earlier killing of four ANC activists who had been abducted and murdered on June 27, 1985. As later revealed, the bodies of these four activists, later known as the "Cradock Four," had been burned and mutilated to avoid detection. This killing

---

28 *TRC Report,* Vol. 5, Chapter 6, p. 202.

29 Name changed in 1993 to C10.

30 I have relied primarily upon Pauw (n 2) and De Kock (n 3) for mandate and background of Vlakplaas.

became one of the defining moments in the struggle against apartheid—*Long Night's Journey into Day* has footage of the funeral service of the "Cradock Four" that was attended by over 60,000 mourners. So concerned were the security police with exposure that the commander of the local detachment, then Colonel Nick Van Rensburg approached De Kock with an order to silence the three policemen. It was De Kock who designed and executed the assassination together with a back-up plan to shoot the deceased with untraceable Eastern Bloc weapons in case they survived the explosion.[31] The incident reveals De Kock's role not only as someone directly involved in secret and illegal activities but as the intermediary between the upper echelons of the state who authorized such actions and the soldiers who implemented them. It was not until the amnesty hearings held in September, 1997 that the nine security police who were involved in the Motherwell bombings came forward to ask for amnesty[32] Of the nine applicants, only De Kock was granted amnesty for the killings—the others were judged to be withholding information and offering inconsistent testimony. During the interrogation of Van Rensburg at his amnesty hearing over the Motherwell bombing, for example, it was De Kock's account of what occurred that was used to test the accuracy of Van Rensburgh's account.[33]

The second incident involved the abduction and murder of Japie Maponya, a security guard, after he either refused or was unable to give information about his brother who had joined the ANC and who was wanted for the murder of a policeman.[34] De Kock arranged the abduction after receiving orders from the head of the local security branch, Colonel Johan Le Roux. Maponya was taken in broad daylight after returning home from work and then thrown into a nearby vehicle where he was blindfolded and covered with a blanket.[35] He was then taken to Vlakplaas where he was interrogated and severely assaulted. According to one witness, "It (the interrogation) went very wild at one stage. When he didn't want to talk, people would stand closer and kick him from all sides."[36] De Kock and another member of his team, Willie Nortje, joined up after the interrogation was in progress. According to other witnesses, De Kock sprayed tear gas into Maponya's mouth. After he still stated that he knew nothing of the whereabouts of his brother, Maponya was given food and pain pills after being manacled to his bed and allowed

---

31   *TRC Reports,* Vol. 6, Chapter 4, p. 79.

32   *TRC Website*, Amnesty Hearings, Port Elizabeth, September 29–October 3, 1997.

33   *TRC Website*, September 29, 1997—General Van Rensburgh, one of the superior officers to whom De Kock reported, is questioned in this hearing for the veracity of his account based on its correspondence with evidence already filed by De Kock.

34   Pauw, p. 49.

35   I have relied on several sources for this account: *TRC Website,* Amnesty Decision, AC/2001/272, February 7, 2001; Evidence given during Amnesty Hearings at Pretoria on July 12 and 15, 1999; *TRC Report,* Vol. 2, Chapter 3, pp. 237–238, Pauw, pp. 49–56; and De Kock, pp. 122–126.

36   Pauw, p. 52.

to sleep through the night. The following morning De Kock called the head office of the security branch to ask what should be done with the prisoner. He received authorization from the commander of the security branch, Colonel Johannes Le Roux, to make Maponya "disappear."[37] That evening De Kock, Nortje, and two others drove Maponya to a nearby farm. Nortje told Maponya to kneel so that he could shoot him in the back of the head. He then struck Maponya with the gun and tried to shoot him. The gun jammed. At this point, De Kock struck Maponya three or four times with the sharp end of a spade cleaving his head open. Nortje then shot Maponya through the head with his pistol. De Kock tried to clear an area with the spade to dig a grave but the underground root system was so knotty and thick that Maponya's body was left in the open covered with a few branches.[38] At his amnesty hearing, De Kock insisted that he had struck Maponya with the spade only to insure that he was dead rather than to "chop him to death" as others had testified. Unlike the Motherwell Four, De Kock was denied amnesty for his participation in this atrocity, presumably because the amnesty committee believed that in this instance he was less credible than the other witnesses. I have recounted this event in some detail in order to show that De Kock was not merely the person who gave the order to engage in acts of violence, he could also be the person who committed the violent acts.

In one of the earliest of the SABC broadcasts on the TRC, De Kock is quoted as describing himself as "apartheid's most effective assassin."[39] Interviews with fellow counterinsurgency personnel characterize him as hardened by battle and immune to the moral inhibitions that afflicted other soldiers. According to Williamson, De Kock stood out as exemplary for his bravery and toughness: "There are people who couldn't complete one tour of six months and ended up suffering from post-traumatic stress disorder. He (De Kock) is a man who was in the frontier for 20 years and a man who was burnt by that 20 years of war."[40] Before becoming commander of operations at Vlakplaas, he had served in one of the first of South Africa's counterinsurgency units, nicknamed Koevoet, where he had earned a reputation for ruthless efficiency. In a documentary on De Kock entitled *Prime Evil,*[41] and released before he became known to the public, he is referred to by his fellow counterinsurgents variously as a "killing machine", as a "very violent war machine, " and as someone who instilled fear in his subordinates. Another member of the hit squad who had participated in some of the assassinations commented that "Gene was a soldier, a killer" and that anyone at Vlakplaas had to learn not to

---

37   *Long Night's Damage,* p. 123.

38   ibid p. 125.

39   *TRC Special Reports,* SABC (South African Broadcasting Corporation) June 16, 1996—all special reports are available online at <http://trc.law.yale.edu/> (last visited on January 17, 2013).

40   *Into the Heart of Darkness,* p. 43.

41   *Prime Evil,* documentary by SABC, 1996. Producer: Jacques Pauw.

feel anything about the killing or "you couldn't do your job."[42] In the testimony given at De Kock's trial as well as at the amnesty hearings, what emerges is a portrait of a community in which moral qualms against killing and the infliction of pain were viewed as weakness and the willingness to engage in violent behavior with no vestiges of remorse was valorized as strength. And it was in this moral hierarchy that, if we accept these characterizations, De Kock was first among the combatants at Vlakplaas not just because he was commander but because he exemplified these qualities of instrumentalism and emotional self-control to a greater degree than anyone else. According to one high-ranking police officer commenting on De Kock's career at Vlakplaas, "I would say he was brilliant in what he achieved for the South African police. He should be regarded as a hero."[43] Indeed, before he was brought to trial, De Kock was the recipient of numerous awards and commendations for exemplary service by the National Party under Presidents P.W. Botha and W. de Klerk.[44] Unlike other claimants who appeared at the amnesty commission, De Kock was forthright in declaring that he had acted out of belief and conviction as an enthusiastic proponent of the government he was charged to defend—"crusader" is the word he chose when asked in an interview how he saw himself during his years at Vlakplaas.[45]

By the time of the amnesty hearings, however, De Kock was already on record for having admitted to almost all the 89 indictments for which he was found guilty after his 18 month trial that began in February, 1995 and culminated in the afore-mentioned verdict.[46] Before the trial, the prosecution had promised immunity and witness protection to several of his closest confederates in return for their highly incriminating testimony. Meanwhile, those who occupied the highest positions of political power during the final years of apartheid had dissociated themselves from the "excesses" of Vlakplaas declaring that De Kock had acted without their authorization.[47] It was under these circumstances in which his former confidants gave evidence against him and his superiors implied that he was a rogue officer

---

42   Quotes taken from documentary, and spoken by Lieutenant Peter Castleton, an officer who was part of Vlakplaas.

43   *Into the Heart of Darkness,* p. 44.

44   See *Long Night's Damage,* pp. 10, 105. De Kock mentions that he received the Police Star for Outstanding Service in 1983 and the SAP (South African Police) Silver Cross for Bravery in 1985, in order to show that the very same acts of violent counterinsurgency for which the leaders of the National Party claimed ignorance during the Goldstone Commission of 1991 and the amnesty hearings were actions for which he received official state commendation.

45   Quoted in Pumla Gobodo-Madikizela, *A Human Being Died That Night—A South African Story of Forgiveness,* Houghton-Miflin, New York, 2003, p. 53.

46   *Into the Heart of Darkness,* pp. 29–31; *A Long Night's Damage,* p. 273.

47   For De Klerk's statement that he was unaware of gross violations of human rights by Vlakplaas, see *TRC Report,* Vol. 5, Chapter 7, p. 264: "I have never condoned gross violations of human rights ... and reject any insinuation that it was ever the policy of my party or government."

that De Kock began to identify the generals and other officials in the chain of command who gave the orders that he had acted upon as head of the Vlakplaas death squad. By criminalizing De Kock's activities as the transgressions of a single individual, the state had placed him outside the reach of the amnesty commission which, as mentioned above, required proof of a political purpose for a claim to be granted. By acknowledging that he had committed all the acts for which he was charged but that they were authorized at the highest level, De Kock sought to attach a political motive to what was being portrayed as criminal misconduct and thereby support his claim for amnesty. When De Kock submitted his 1,000-page application[48] to the amnesty committee just 30 minutes before the deadline, it could be argued as the SABC suggested in its first video broadcast of the hearings that both his confession and disclosure were merely strategic moves in a final desperate attempt to escape prison or, as described in the broadcast, he was "trying to save his neck by implicating his superiors."[49]

But it was not De Kock as master strategist but rather De Kock as convert from the most predatory of counterinsurgents to remorseful confessor that would prove to be the most contentious of claims in the transition from apartheid to the new democratic South Africa. In a number of highly publicized encounters both on-stage at the hearings and off-stage in private encounters later to be disclosed to the public in books, articles, and news items, De Kock presented himself as a man who had undergone a fundamental shift in his being from someone who had fought ruthlessly and passionately against the ANC and its allies to someone who now despised and condemned his own behavior. But, as I have argued above, remorse is not an emotion that is claimed so much as attributed. Validation by others is the necessary complement to the transgressor's moral performance. And, especially in the extra-judicial context of the TRC, the encounters critical to this process of validation were even more visible and public than in the court records and judgments discussed in early chapters. It was not merely De Kock who was exposed to the close scrutiny of the public and the press—so also were those who affirmed his transformation. So substantial were the meanings attached to whether or not his remorse was credible or sufficient that the very act of recognition became as divisive as whether or not De Kock deserved amnesty in the first place.

Apart from the statement quoted at the outset of this chapter, De Kock made a number of other equally categorical speeches denouncing the activities of the National Party in general and his own actions in particular. At his trial, for example, he had told the court when he spoke in mitigation of his sentence court:

> I cannot say how dirty one feels. Whatever we attempted in the interests of the country did not work. All we did was to injure people, to leave people with

---

48 "De Kock Hands in Amnesty Application," May 10, 1997, *SAPA* gives the length as 1,000 pages; Payne (n 20) p. 255 gives 4,000 pages as the length.

49 *TRC Special Reports,* June 16, 1996.

unforgivable pain, to leave behind children who will never know their parents. I sympathize with the victims as if they were my own children.[50]

Even more important, however, was the direct validation by victims and their surrogates. Most notable was his direct encounter with the widows of the Motherwell Four, who would later become among the strongest advocates in his request for amnesty and later, after the expiry of the TRC, in his efforts to secure a pardon. At the amnesty hearings held in Port Elizabeth on September 29, 1997, De Kock spoke to them through his lawyer who asked why he had found it necessary to give evidence on this occasion. De Kock replied that he had two reasons—one, to "expose the people who gave the orders," and "also to display my sympathy and empathy with the families."[51] This led to a meeting with the victims, one of whom offered the following description of her interaction with De Kock:

> I was profoundly touched by him, especially when he said he wished he could bring our husbands back. I didn't even look at him when he was speaking …
>
> Yet I felt the genuineness in his apology. I couldn't control my tears. I could hear him, but I was overwhelmed by emotion, and I was just nodding, as a way of saying, yes, I forgive you, I hope that when he sees our tears, he knows that they are not only tears for our husbands, but tears for him as well. … I would like to show him that there is a future, and that he can still change.[52]

Equally significant was his meeting with journalist Jann Turner, who was highly visible both as a TV reporter for SABC covering the hearings and as herself a victim whose activist anti-apartheid father had been assassinated in 1978— Turner was a child when her father was shot and she was the first to find him wounded and dying, and then unable to be resuscitated. She agreed to see De Kock after receiving an invitation through his lawyer to visit him in prison. Like the Motherwell widows, Turner was moved by her encounter:

> I barely recognized the haggard, thin, depressed and disoriented man the warders brought in. He talked about dying, he seemed to feel he deserved to die. That day I sensed he was changing fundamentally. There is nothing like staring at the prospect of life in jail to make a person reflect searchingly on what has put them there. I believe that is what De Kock had begun to do. He was overwhelmed by regret, he felt his life had been a destructive waste and he was angry with himself for being naïve enough to believe.[53]

---

50   *Long Night's Damage*, pp. 274–275.

51   *TRC Website,* Amnesty Hearing at Port Elizabeth on September 29, 1997.

52   Pumla Gobodo-Madikizela, "Remorse, Rehumanization, and Forgiveness," Vol. 42, no. 1, 2002, *Journal of Humanistic Psychology,* p. 17.

53   Jann Turner, "Eugene: From Apocalypse Now to Scotland the Brave," *Mail & Guardian Online* at <http://mg.co.za/article/1999-05-28-eugene-from-apocalypse-now-to-

As persons whose lives had been directly affected by the violence of apartheid, victims at the TRC occupied a privileged position not just as those entitled to forgive the transgressor but also as arbiters of whether the remorse shown was genuine.[54] Now, here were the voices of those whose husbands had been murdered by De Kock and another who was witness to her father's death at a tender age all corroborating that he was what he appeared to be—someone suffering both emotionally and physically for his wrongs and whose pain came not from distress over his own predicament of lifelong incarceration but from empathy with those whose suffering he had caused.

But it was the work of Pumla Gobodo-Madikizela, a psychologist who also served as member of the Human Rights Committee of the TRC, that more than any other single contribution to the discussion about De Kock set the terms of debate over the credibility and sufficiency of his transformation. Gobodo-Madikizela's monograph entitled *A Human Being Died That Night: A South African Story of Forgiveness* was based on the 46 interviews she conducted with De Kock over three months in 1997, while he was serving time in a maximum security prison in Pretoria. The work is an account not just of De Kock's moral struggle to acknowledge and take responsibility for the harm he had caused but, equally relevant for present purposes, the author's own moral struggle over how to respond to these revelations. Against the dominant representation of De Kock as Prime Evil—as someone whose identity was subsumed under his violent history— Gobodo-Madikizela conceived of De Kock as the perpetrator of acts of radical evil but as someone not wholly defined by those acts. What separated him from other mass murderers in the service of dehumanizing ideologies was his remorse. Without the sure presence of these feelings, she argued, De Kock could make no moral claim on us, no claim to mercy, nor claim for any of the other benefits that come with what she refers to as rehumanization. Remorse is what made De Kock worthy of forgiveness: "Forgiveness usually begins with the person who needs to be forgiven. This means that there must be something in the perpetrator's behavior, some 'sign' that invites the victim's forgiveness. The most crucial sign is the expression of remorse."[55]

But how could one verify that De Kock's feelings were real and not the "'witness stand' remorse that suddenly is forthcoming because, with no way out, the accused wants moral leniency?"[56] And how must this remorse be shown by someone who has committed extreme transgressions? Gobodo-Madikizela's book

---

scotland-the> (last accessed on January 19, 2013).

54   Michael Humphrey, "From Victim to Victimhood: Truth Commission and Trials as Rituals of Political Transition and Individual Healing," Vol. 14:2, 2003, *Australian Journal of Anthropology,* pp. 171–187. As Humphrey observes, "the spectacle of the victim's pain and suffering in truth commissions and trials seeks to undo the original spectacle of violence, the atrocity … ," p. 173.

55   *A Human Being Died That Night,* p. 98.

56   ibid p. 125.

takes its title from the encounter that changed her perception of De Kock and that led her to believe that his remorse was real. Here, De Kock is recounting an incident in which he has just completed an assignment in which he helped murder ANC operatives in Lesotho and he begins to experience a smell on the way home. By the time he has arrived at his home, the smell has become unbearable and he takes off his clothes, puts them in a pile and goes straight for the shower. After the first shower, he towels himself dry and realizes the smell was still clinging to his body. Then he takes off his clothes and puts them in the garbage along with the towel. And, while he is telling this story, his facial muscles are contorted as if he is reliving the experience of revulsion at that moment: "His gestures had become extreme, he motioned in an exaggerated way, his eyes bulging, pulling at this arms as if he were struggling to remove something attacking his flesh, something undetachable from his skin."[57] It is this encounter that Gobodo-Madikizela points to as both the moment when De Kock's conscience stirred and was then silenced in Lesotho finally to be reawakened and felt once again: "At that moment I thought I saw a man finally acknowledging the debt he owed to his conscience."[58] In this account, "true" remorse becomes the involuntary suffering that the transgressor displays on their body—the flooding out of feelings, the helplessness of loss of control, the showing of the pain rather than speaking it. In this and a few other encounters, the author described her subject as breaking down as he began to recognize what he had done, as, for example, when he recalled his meeting with the Motherwell widows and "His mouth quivered and there were tears in his eyes. As he started to speak, his hand trembled and he became visibly distressed."[59] Extreme transgression called for extreme suffering. In the narratives of Gobodo-Madikizela especially, but also in Turner's account, there is the portrait of a man whose moral transformation is inscribed on his body—he is someone who has suffered and is suffering for his wrongs and he is no longer the same person he was.

But if at core De Kock could now be understood as not so different from ourselves—if his deepest emotional response to his actions corresponded to the visceral feelings of revulsion and self-condemnation that all members of the moral community should experience towards such transgressions—if, in short, he was at his emotional core just like us, then were we not like him? Having established a congruence between herself and De Kock, Gobodo-Madikizela elaborates on the implications of this congruence. If we can say that De Kock had narrowed the moral distance between himself and his victims through a sharing of similar sensibilities towards his extreme transgression, then perhaps the distance between ourselves and De Kock's previous incarnation was also not as great as we would imagine. If we could no longer—by benefit of acknowledging his remorse—mark him as irreducibly different in his moral emotions from the rest of us, then how can

57   ibid p. 51.

58   ibid.

59   Gobodo-Madikizela, "Remorse, Forgiveness, and Rehumanization: Stories from South Africa," pp. 21–22.

we be sure we would not have succumbed to the same influences and behaved the same way were we in similar circumstances? Or, as the author states, "That one is not confronted with the choices De Kock could have or could not have made, that one was not a member of the privileged class in apartheid South Africa are matters of sheer grace."[60]

If by benefit of his remorse, we could no longer disown De Kock as an outcast from our moral community, then what he was before his transformation—the violent, crusading defender of apartheid— differed in degree and not in kind from what we might be under the same circumstances. For Gobodo-Madikizela, humanizing De Kock or admitting him to the moral community of the new post-apartheid South Africa meant that his deep complicity with the evil of apartheid was made possible by the lesser complicity of all those who did not actively oppose it. If someone with a capacity for genuine remorse could allow their conscience to die, then none of us were safe from the coarsening effects of adverse conditions. On the other hand, if the person who most embodied the cruelty and violence of apartheid could be forgiven, then no one was beyond forgiveness—provided they were genuinely remorseful.

But, because the showing of remorse is necessarily a performance that requires an audience, there is always an element of artifice in how it is communicated no matter how deeply felt the emotion. After all, De Kock had sought out certain of his victims but not others—Japie Maponya's widow and brothers were never approached, for example, to engage in private dialogue over his murder nor were the many others who survived the death of their husbands, children, or parents. One of Maponya's brothers had attended De Kock's trial and had described him as without remorse in an interview—"When you look at him, he didn't have any sorry. He was not having that shame."[61] Had De Kock selected as his audience only those whom he sensed would be most receptive to his recantations? And why were Jann Turner or Pumla Gobodo-Madikizela chosen as gatekeepers to the moral community and not others? During one of their encounters, De Kock had asked with apparent trepidation whether any of Gobodo-Madikizela's relatives had been among his victims.[62] She replied in the negative, but did this absence of direct victimization qualify or disqualify her as the moral arbiter who could credit or discredit De Kock's claim to be remorseful and who might encourage or discourage acts of forgiveness?

Without the institutional protections afforded by the law, those who step forward in support or in opposition to a claim to remorse assume some of the same risks as the transgressor. What is at stake in the attribution of remorse is not only the credibility of the transgressor but also the credibility of the gatekeeper. Gobodo-Madikizela refers to a question directed at her after presenting her work on De Kock to a psychoanalytic conference suggesting that she may have been

---

60　*A Human Being Died That Night,* p. 57.

61　*Into the Heart of Darkness,* p. 51.

62　*A Human Being Died That Night,* p. 114.

manipulated—a question she in fact had anticipated.[63] Both she and Turner also mention having to dispel suspicions from friends and colleagues that they were attracted to or fascinated by De Kock—allegations that called into question their judgment and their objectivity. One colleague had commented to Gobodo-Madikizela after hearing about her work: "He must be a very good-looking man."[64] However well they dealt with these attempts at debunking and however unfair the sexual innuendoes, the voicing of such suspicions is an indication of the informal moral policing that occurs when the community is divided over whether or not to grant a transgressor recognition as a moral entity with all the benefits that come with that recognition. If De Kock were genuinely remorseful, then his suffering and anguish over his transgressions became a fit object for compassion even and especially from his victims. But if he were feigning or otherwise incapable of experiencing remorse, such sympathy was misplaced at best and an act of apology or condonation of extreme violence at worst.[65]

Gobodo-Madikizela recognized these risks in her discussion of her own moral struggle over how much social distance to maintain in her growing relationship with her subject. Not to respond to his pain and suffering was to contribute to his dehumanization, but to acknowledge his pain while overlooking his record of extreme violence was to succumb to identification. Her efforts to achieve this balance may be taken as a kind of moral self-policing to maintain her own credibility as a moral arbiter. The risk of validation is that instead of elevating the moral status of the transgressor, it will diminish the moral authority of the gatekeeper. Alliance with someone who claims remorse but who is perceived as opportunistic and strategic exposes the arbiter to the charge of complicity with those who have betrayed the moral community—all the more degrading in the case of extreme transgressions.

But doubts about De Kock's credibility arose less from questioning the motives of those who supported his claim to personal transformation than from the articulation of other narratives that read strikingly different meanings into his demonstrations of remorse. No one was more public in advancing such a narrative than Jacques Pauw, a well-known South African journalist who was a co-founder in 1988 of the only Afrikaner newspaper that spoke out against apartheid and who made the documentary *Prime Evil*. The person that emerged from the film and

---

63   ibid p. 45.

64   ibid pp. 122–123.

65   As an example of this informal public policing of when expressions of remorse should be credited and by implication, humanized, consider this response to Sereny's above-cited work on Albert Speer: "In humanizing monsters, Sereny was a major force in in creating a very modern and corrosive ideology that architects of evil should not be punished but understood and even rewarded to help them atone for their sins." See Tom Bower, *Daily Mail Online*, "The woman who tried to humanize a monster," June 30, 2012 at <s.dailymail. co.uk/news/article-2161909/Gitta-Sereny-The-woman-tried-humanise-monsters.html> (last visited on January 19, 2012).

writings of Pauw was a "heartless, cold-blooded killer"[66]—someone about whom Pauw could say after several interviews: "Only Eugene de Kock will know whether or not he really feels remorse for his victims. He has never shown any compassion for any of those he killed or tortured and I have often wondered: did this man enjoy killing people?"[67] In Pauw's rendering, De Kock showed remorse only after he had exhausted all means to protect himself and to preserve apartheid, "ultimately, De Kock made war until the bitter end. He didn't stop when the ANC was unbanned, but continued to kill, plotted to derail a fragile peace and tried to uphold an unjust system."[68] In this representation, actions and being cohere, De Kock is the assassin whose evil deeds are a true reflection of his callous instrumentalism. Nor does Pauw view De Kock as merely the inevitable product of his Afrikaner origins. If others as white Afrikaners had grown up in similar circumstances and were nevertheless able to detach themselves from an immoral system, why could De Kock not have done likewise, he would ask.[69] Just as De Kock stood apart even from the other assassins at Vlakplaas in his absence of compassion, so he stood outside the moral community as someone radically different from those around him. Regarding the credibility of De Cock's recantation, Pauw would observe during the amnesty hearings: "He (De Kock) was very arrogant until he was convicted. On that very day, De Kock changed his whole strategy. He became a man obsessed by remorse."[70] What Gobodo-Madikileza perceived as De Kock's fundamental shift in his feelings for what he had done, Pauw saw as a moral performance that was both feigned and strategic. For Pauw, De Kock had not changed so much as proven that he was adept at whatever he did whether as a "political serial killer" or as a penitent convert to belief in a multiracial South Africa.

In this and in later debates about the fate of De Kock, the issue of remorse would remain one of the primary sites of conflict not only over whether he should be forgiven and released from prison, but also over the moral boundaries of the new South Africa. When, in January, 2010, there were reports that he was about to be pardoned by President Jacob Zuma, De Kock would once again be the object of close scrutiny with those who had found him remorseful and who had forgiven him now supporting his bid for freedom and those alleging that he lacked remorse demanding that he not be released.[71] As someone reborn and transformed, he

---

66   Jacques Pauw, *Dances with Devils: A Journalist's Search for Truth*, Cape Town, Zebra Press, 2006, p. 143.

67   *Into the Heart of Darkness*, p. 174.

68   ibid. p. 147

69   *Dances with Devils*, p. 16.

70   Article for this quote cited in Payne, p. 266, Darren Schuettler: "Eugene de Kock's last Desperate Attempt to be Freed from his Crimes," *Star*, June 15, 1999.

71   For examples of articles that opposed his pardon on grounds that he had not shown remorse, see Mia Swart, "Remorseless De Kock is Just Where he Belongs, *All Africa, AFNWS,* January 20, 2010 and Christi Ven Der Westhuizen, "White Power at work: no pardon for De Kock," *Mail & Guardian Online* at <http://mg.co.za/article/2010-01-15-white-power-at-work-no-pardon-for-de-kock> (last visited on January 19, 2013). For

could expect that his own suffering and privations would be acknowledged and that his claim to mercy given serious consideration no matter how grave his earlier transgressions. But, if he were without remorse, as others continued to assert, it was an insult even to contemplate an offer of pardon. At stake as well were the rival conceptions of the history of apartheid. Was De Kock the criminal as depicted at trial, the fearsome assassin as described in *Prime Evil*, who was unaffected by the inner stirrings of conscience that would inhibit ordinary people, or was he no different from other South Africans whose conscience had been quashed by social processes made visible only after the termination of apartheid?

Meanwhile, De Kock had told Turner after his meeting with her "You see, the only friends I have now are my former enemies.[72]" A few years later, in 2002, when Gobodo-Madikizela had visited him at Pretoria prison, she learned that De Kock had requested a transfer from the section that housed inmates who had fought for apartheid to the section that contained former members of the ANC and the PAC.[73] He would later credit his survival in the harsh confines of prison in part to the interventions of black inmates. As with other converts from one moral community to another, De Kock would go on to be ostracized by his former comrades while never winning the complete trust of those to whom he would give his allegiance.

Remorse and Forgiveness

When the subject of his pardon came up, De Kock was quoted as asking a question the irony of which he himself may not have appreciated: "Is there some kind of sliding scale to show how sorry you are?"[74] To which we might respond—based on the foregoing analysis—that indeed, there is a moral economy in many if not all jurisdictions in which the greater the perceived transgression, the more exacting the requirements to demonstrate that the remorse is genuine. But, we would also have to add, it is a moral economy the currency of which is subject to continual fluctuation and always open to contestation.

It is easy to see why De Kock's efforts to shift allegiance from one moral community to another captivated the South African public. It was almost as if he were enacting on his person the transition from the maximally racialized society

---

new items that support his pardon and describe him as remorseful, see Pumla Gobodo-Madikizela, "Toward an Anatomy of Violence," *Mail & Guardian Online,* January 15, 2010 at <http://mg.co.za/article/2010-01-15-towards-an-anatomy-of-violence> (last visited on January 19, 2013), and "Free De Kock—widows Victims' wives push Zuma to pardon Prime Evil," *Saturday Star,* January 23, 2010, p. 1.

72   Turner (n 53).

73   *A Human Being Died That Night,* p. 136.

74   Nico Geldenhuys, "De Kock will not give up," March 1, 2010, *News 24,* online at <http://m.news24.com/news24/SouthAfrica/News/De-Kock-will-not-give-up-20100228> (last accessed on January 20, 2013).

under apartheid to the multiracial democracy as contemplated under the new constitution. As Director of Operations for Vlakplaas, he had occupied one of the most politically sensitive yet vital positions for the protection of apartheid in the face of growing opposition from within and outside South Africa. It was a role that he fully inhabited, including its demands that he subordinate all ethical inhibitions against murder, deceit, or exploitation of the vulnerable to the higher duty of sacrifice for one's country. Through his demonstrations of remorse, he performed the anguished and painful transition from chief technician at Vlakplaas to aspiring member of the new society. His inward journey paralleled the changes that were occurring outside. The very actions that before had conferred pride and respect now became sources of shame and self-loathing. De Kock's remorse was manifested through a mortification of the self that had palpable physical signs of trembling, tears, and the flooding of emotions usually kept private. This relinquishing of the former self was then followed by attempts to reach out to former victims signifying his conversion from one moral community to another.

But the same process by which the transgressor reinstates or in this case establishes membership in a moral community is also the process by which membership is barred. Those who opposed De Kock's pardon or wished to withhold forgiveness found it necessary as well to debunk his claims to remorse. There was no room in public discourse to credit him with remorse without also supporting his claim to forgiveness. The contestation over the authenticity of De Kock's remorse was simultaneously a debate over the limits of forgiveness and the penetrability or impenetrability of the barriers to reconciliation between former adversaries.

But there is another dimension to remorse apart from its didactic role in instructing the community for which actions and beliefs you are obliged to feel remorse. The enactment of remorse requires that the transgressor bear full responsibility for the wrongs that have been committed even when, as in the defense of apartheid, these wrongs were authorized by government and tacitly acquiesced to by those who supported the government. In looking at how expressions of remorse and their validation shape the moral architecture of society, the silences become as significant as the spectacles. That the persons who authorized De Kock's actions never came forward, nor were obliged to demonstrate remorse reveals the political limits of moral accountability. Just as the spectacle of remorse instructs the community about the moral requirements of membership, it also communicates that in addition to the demand for moral accountability, there is also a space for moral impunity and that this space is reserved for those in the community who hold the greatest power.

Chapter 6
The Social and Legal Regulation
of Remorse

A half century after his participation as a lawyer specializing in the newly emerging field of war crimes during the Nuremberg trials, Benjamin Ferencz would confide to author Erna Paris in the course of her magisterial investigation into the memory traces left by the atrocities of the twentieth century what stood out from his encounters with the Nazi defendants. He referred to one exchange in particular—his interview with Otto Ohlendorf, the head of one of the notorious Einsatzgruppen divisions responsible for the extermination of Jews in the territories occupied by Germany during World War II. Asked to describe his activities when carrying out the killing of some 90,000 Jewish men, women, and children in Ukraine, what astonished Ferencz was that unlike so many of the other defendants, Ohlendorf made no effort to conceal or understate his role in the killings. While such absence of guile might be taken as a commendable desire to fulfill his oath of truth telling before the court, it became clear that what really distinguished Ohlendorf from his fellow defendants was his complete lack of self-reproach. When questioned about why he had carried out these executions, he replied, "Because it is inconceivable to me that a subordinate leader should not carry out orders given by the leaders of the state."[1] In a final encounter in which Ferencz inquired whether he had any last words to impart to his family or to the court before his execution, Ohlendorf answered, "The Jews in America will suffer for what you have done to me."[2] Even with full knowledge of his zealous compliance with the genocidal program of the Nazis, it was Ohlendorf's absence of remorse that made his actions appear even more shocking to Ferencz.

It is with such reactions to the presence or absence of remorse that I began this book and it is these events that remain the bedrock data with which I have worked in each of the succeeding chapters. Whether in the popular revulsion and consternation at Timothy McVeigh's refusal to demonstrate remorse or in the intense and prolonged public debate in South Africa over whether Eugene de Kock's demonstrations of remorse were credible or the many other examples discussed above, the thrust of the preceding analysis has been to make visible the social processes through which communities seek to achieve among their members an alignment of their inner feelings about transgression. I have suggested that it is through this process of the

---

1   Erna Paris, *Long Shadows—Truth, Lies, and History*, Vintage Canada: Toronto, 2001, pp. 442–443.

2   ibid.

setting of expectations over what acts should require remorse and how remorse should be demonstrated that groups constitute themselves as moral communities, that is, communities that are bound by a shared moral sensibility about when and how to feel remorse. Whatever Lieutenant William Calley may have experienced in 1970 in the immediate aftermath of the My Lai incident, it is clear from the public response at that time that he was not expected to feel or to demonstrate remorse. By 2009, however, those who had lost their lives in the incident had been redefined as persons whose suffering mattered and Lt. Calley's show of remorse for his role in these events was expected and accepted. It was the utter absence of remorse in Colonel De Kock's demeanor that bolstered his credibility as a leader at Vlakplaas when he implemented the numerous assassinations, disappearances, and official untruths that were central to the operations of the secret organization. By the time of the Truth and Reconciliation Commission, the actions that had earned De Kock his promotions had been redefined as atrocities and the persons murdered were now part of the moral community whose violent deaths were expected to elicit feelings of remorse.

Yet it is not only during the rapid transitions that take place when a country moves from peace to war, or when one regime is succeeded by the group it sought to repress that the work that goes into creating, sustaining, and transforming moral communities comes to the surface. There are also those occasions when the imagined alignment between the court and the community can no longer be upheld as exemplified in the case of Robert Latimer. Here the gap in perception between the legal construction of Latimer as a convicted murderer and the public representation of his act as benevolent and altruistic generated a clash of expectations over whether he should feel remorse and how it should be demonstrated. The result of this misalignment, as we saw, was that the parole board relinquished its demand that Latimer show remorse in exchange for his freedom. It is at these moments of public spectacle when individuals are forced to shift between moral communities that have radically different expectations for their members or where there is a major reconfiguration of the multiple moral communities that comprise a modern society or where there is a profound and unresolvable gap between the state and civil society over who is a member of the moral community, that the work of the court and the community in creating new norms for when remorse is expected or not expected is most discernible. Yet, from the vantage point of this inquiry, these occurrences are merely the most extreme manifestations of the continuing social processes by which a community defines which acts will count as transgressions and, if transgressions, what moral sensibility will have to be demonstrated to reestablish the wrongdoer as a member of the moral community. It is in the language of these mundane exchanges whether formalized as in law or less formalized as in the communication of approval or disapproval by a moral community that we decide when remorse is expected, how it should be expressed, and whose suffering should occasion this expression and whose need not.

But it is the intensity as well as the ubiquity of these reactions that has been at the forefront of this inquiry. The more grave the transgression, the more urgent and impassioned the scrutiny directed to the character of the wrongdoer. Conceiving of the offender as remorseful reimagines them as a member of our own moral community—as someone with whom we share a sensibility and as someone who is able to suffer for the wrongs they have done as we imagine we might suffer if we were to commit those wrongs. Placing the offender in the category of the remorseless does more than negate their claim to mitigation or mercy. How a wrongdoer feels towards their misconduct is as important in terms of its public representation as the act itself—one of the recurring questions in crimes that are perceived as violent and desecrating is whether the offender has ever felt remorse for their actions. So deeply entrenched and visceral are the reactions of those who belong to the moral community, that the inability of a perpetrator to feel remorse under these extreme circumstances is perceived not merely as a betrayal of community but as a deficiency that separates them from the rest of humanity. As we have seen in Chapter 3 above, it is the imputation of remorselessness that is enough to persuade an otherwise uncertain juror to vote for death and it is the absence of remorse that converts the "psychopath" into someone who is ineluctably different from the rest of us. As Durkheim taught us a century ago, societies are bound together not just by allegiance to common values, but by shared sentiments.[3] The impassioned expectation that members of the same moral community will feel remorse for the same action and the outrage directed at those who do not, especially when coupled with the power of the state to punish or to mitigate or the power of the group to exclude or include, I take as evidence of the paramount importance that is attached to adherence to these "feeling rules."

It has been equally central to this analysis to observe how this involvement by court and community affects the moral performances through which remorse or its absence is communicated. As we have seen, it is the very power of this characterization as remorseful or remorseless to humanize or dehumanize the wrongdoer that casts suspicion on its public expression. To succeed in this

---

3   The debt to Durkheim is not for his view that moral uniformity is the mark of a normally functioning society or that law expresses the will of the collectivity. But while these assumptions have been critiqued for over 50 years, they do not detract from Durkheim's overall achievement whose counter-intuitive vision of the relationship between transgression and social order continues to inspire succeeding generations of thinkers. Applying his vision to the analysis above, we can still argue that the quest for remorse and the testing of its credibility is a boundary-defining moment for the multiple moral communities that inhabit the same geography and are subject to the same regimes of power. Indeed, it is possible to suggest that the intensity of reaction when expectations are not met helps to make visible the emotional substrate that Durkheim believed to lay at the foundation of society as a moral order. See David Garland, *Punishment and Modern Society: A Study in Social Theory,* University of Chicago Press, 1990, especially pp. 23–82, for what is still one of the most important efforts to separate those parts of Durkheim's vision that continue to be relevant for modern social inquiry from those that can no longer be supported.

performance, we demand from the wrongdoer that it is the stirrings of conscience and not fear of consequences that prompted his or her feelings of self-condemnation. But because the performance can lead to a benefit, we are never fully convinced of its veracity. Hence, the omnipresence of skeptical counter-narratives to negate claims to genuine remorse as described above.

Yet, there is more to this potential for discreditation than simply the gnawing suspicion of dissimulation. So resonant and richly connotative is the imputation of remorsefulness that it imposes obligations on the community that confers it. As we saw in Chapter 3, prosecutors in cases of capital punishment in the United States were virtually uniform in their determination to invalidate claims to remorse advanced by the offender or their advocates at every level of legal contestation. In increasing the sentence of Mr. R. in Chapter 2, we observed that the appeal court found it necessary to reject the conclusion of the lower court that his remorse was genuine. What this suggests is that at least in practice if not in law, the coupling of remorse and mitigation works in both directions—that it is not just that mitigation or mercy demands a show of remorse but that a show of remorse that is validated as sincere obliges the state to dispense mercy or to offer mitigation. Indeed, as we have seen in the far more informal workings of the TRC, so powerful is the narrative that relates remorse to redemption and reconciliation that similar obligations were pressed upon victims to forgive perpetrators if the perpetrator was believed to have demonstrated remorse.[4]

It is this coupling of remorse and mitigation then that leads to the conundrum[5] that the state must find no remorse in the wrongdoer if it is not prepared to mitigate the punishment. Those who receive the ultimate penalties of the state must be found not only guilty but also morally unworthy by invalidating any claim they may have to feelings of remorse for their wrongdoings. The unknowability of feelings of remorse and the irreducible ambiguity in the way such feelings are measured and authenticated lends itself to this process of nihilation or erasure of the perpetrator as moral entity. No matter what emotional acrobatics the wrongdoer performs, the standard for what counts as "true remorse" can always be raised to exceed that which has been shown. Hence the validity of the insight underlying De Kock's earlier cited lament: "Is there some kind of sliding scale for showing how sorry you are?" Whether or not a moral performance is successful depends on the weight that the community attaches to the transgression.

It is at this awkward juncture that one can situate the necessary but always provisional ritual of showing remorse. It is in the expectation over when remorse is

---

4   As discussed in Annalise Acorn, *Compulsory Compassion: A Critique of Restorative Justice,* UBC Press, Vancouver, 2004, and Claire Moon, *op. cit.,* 2008.

5   I have made this point elsewhere in "Coupling and Decoupling Remorse and Forgiveness in Legal Discourse," in *Forgiveness— Promise, Possibility, and Failure,* 2009, Inter-Disciplinary Press at <https://www.interdisciplinarypress.net/online-store/ebooks/ethos-and-modern-life/forgiveness-promise-possibility-and-failure> last visited on April 22, 2013.

to be felt and demonstrated as well as in the expectation over when those feelings are to be silenced that we can locate the passions that hold groups together, that pull them apart, and that divide them from each other. In confronting these expectations, the transgressor is caught between the overt demand to be genuine and the covert demand to surrender emerging from the encounter sometimes defiant, sometimes broken, and sometimes transformed.

Bibliography

I have divided the bibliography into three parts. Part I cites the databases used in the text. Part II includes books and articles cited in the text. Part III includes judicial opinions cited in the text.

Part I

I am indebted to the following online databases for portions of the above analysis. First, I have relied upon *LexisNexis* for the retrieval and selection of legal judgments for analysis in Chapter 2 and 3. Second, I have made extensive use of *Factiva* to retrieve Canadian media coverage of the trial of Robert Latimer in Chapter 4. Third, I relied on the official Truth and Reconciliation website at <http://www.justice.gov.za/trc/> for retrieving the documents necessary for my analysis in Chapter 5.

Part II

Abbott A., 2001. "Into the mind of a killer." *Nature,* 410, March 15, 296–298.

Abbott K., 2001. "Witness: 'It's Over' Timothy McVeigh has not Last Words but Stares Straight into Camera Before Dying." *Rocky Mountain News,* 2A.

Acorn A., 2004. *Compulsory Compassion: A Critique of Restorative Justice.* Vancouver: University of British Columbia Press.

Adams R., with Hoffer W. and Hoffer M.M., 1991. *Adams v. Texas.* New York: St. Martin's Press.

Ahmed S., 2004. *The Cultural Politics of Emotion.* New York: Routledge.

Arab P., 2007. "Latimer victimized for lack of remorse." *Calgary Herald,* December 14, A28.

Arrigo B.A. and Shipley S., 2001. "The Confusion over Psychopathy (I): Historical Considerations." *International Journal of Offender Therapy and Comparative Criminology,* 45, 325–344.

Athens L., 1995. "Dramatic Self-Change." *Sociological Quarterly,* 36 (3), Summer, 571–586.

Bajaric M. and Amarkkehara K., 2001. "Feeling Sorry? Tell Someone Who Cares: The Uselessness of Remorse in Sentencing." *Howard Journal* 40, 364–376.

Bandes S., ed., 1999. *The Passions of the Law.* New York: New York University Press.

Bauslaugh G., 2010. *Robert Latimer.* Toronto, James Lorimer.

Bennett C., 2008. *The Apology Ritual: A Philosophical Theory of Punishment.* Cambridge: Cambridge University Press.

Bernstein H., 1967. *The World That Was Ours.* London: Heinemann.

Blair J., Mitchell D. and Blair K., 2005. *The Psychopath: Emotion and the Brain.* Malden, Massachusetts: Blackwell.

Blank S., 2006. "Killing Time: The Process of Waiving Appeal: The Michael Ross Death Penalty Cases." *Journal of Law and Social Policy* 14, 735–777.

Blatchford C., 2009. "I have myself to blame for the decision I made that night." *Globe and Mail,* September 18, A12.

Bourke J., 1999. *An Intimate History of Killing: Face-to-Face in 20th-Century Warfare.* New York: Basic Books.

BradBerry G., 2001. "Victim's Families come face-to-face with killer—McVeigh execution. *The Times,* 4.

Brooks P. and Gewirtz P., eds, 1996. *Law's Stories: Narrative and Rhetoric in the Law.* New Haven: Yale University Press.

Camus A., 1989. *The Stranger*—Trans. by Matthew Ward. New York: Alfred Knopf.

Canadian Press, 2011. "Melissa Todorovic, Teen Murderer, Moving to Adult Jail." *Huffington Post Canada,* December 22, 1.

Chang Y., 2001. *Culture and Communication: An Ethnographic Study of Chinese Courtroom Communications.* PhD Thesis, University of Iowa, unpublished.

Cleckley H., 1976. *The Mask of Sanity,* 5th edition. St. Louis: C.V. Mosby and Co.

Coetzee J.M., 1999. *Disgrace.* Secker and Warburg.

Cole B., 1997. "Latimer leniency wrong message." *Winnipeg Free Press,* December 2, A13.

Costanzo M. and Peterson J., 1994. "Attorney Persuasion in the Capital Penalty Phase: A Content Analysis of Closing Arguments." *Journal of Social Issues,* 50, 125–147.

Council of Canadians with Disabilities (CCD) "Latimer Watch" <http://www.ccdonline.ca/en/humanrights/endoflife/latimer/1996/11> Last visited on December 27, 2012.

Covey R.D., 2009. "Criminal Madness: Cultural Iconography and Insanity." *Stanford Law Review,* 61, 1375–1428.

Cox M., ed., 1999. *Remorse and Reparation.* London: Jessica Kingsley Publications.

Dahlberg L., 2009. "Emotional Tropes in the Courtroom: On Representation of Affect and Emotion in Legal Court Proceedings." *Nordic Theater Studies* 21, 129–152.

De Kock E., 1998. *A Long Night's Damage.* Saxonwold, South Africa: Contra Press.

Diagnostic and Statistical Manual of Mental Disorder: DSM-IV-TR, 4th ed., text revision, 2000. Washington, D.C.: American Psychiatric Association.

Duff A., 2001. *Punishment, Communication, and Community.* New York: Oxford University Press.

Duncan M.G., 2002. "'So Young and So Untender': Remorseless Children and the Expectations of the Law." *Columbia Law Review,* 102, no. 6, 1469–1526.

Downie J., 2004. *Dying Justice: A Case for Decriminalizing Euthanasia and Assisted Suicide in Canada.* Toronto: University of Toronto Press.

—— Editorial, December 6, 2007. "A terrible decision on Robert Latimer." *Globe and Mail,* A22.

— — Editorial, December 6, 2007. "Latimer Deserved Parole." *Toronto Star,* AAO6.

— — Editorial, December 7, 2007. "A Justifiable Decision—Lack of Remorse Sufficient to Deny Parole for Latimer." *Calgary Herald,* A26.

—— Editorial, December 7, 2007. "Parole Latimer." *Montreal Gazette,* A18.

—— Editorial, February 29, 2008. "A line crossed." *Winnipeg Free Press,* A10.

—— Editorial, August 28, 2009. *New York Times,* A22.

Eisenberg T., Garvey S.P. and Wells M.T. , 1998. "But Was He Sorry? The Role of Remorse in Capital Sentencing." *Cornell Law Review,* 83, pp. 1599–1637.

Ellis H., 1890. *The Criminal.* London: Walter Scott.

Fagan D., 1988. "Lawyer says little done in 'futile' Marshall Case." *Globe and Mail,* January 15, p. A5.

Fagan K., 2001. "McVeigh Shows No Remorse." *San Francisco Chronicle,* June 11, A1.

Fagan K. and Squatrigila C., June 12, 2001. "Death of a Terrorist: McVeigh offers no last words, only a steely stare for his victims." *San Francisco Chronicle,* p. A1.

Federman C., Holmes D. and Jacob J.D., 2009. "Deconstructing the Psychopath: A Critical Discursive Analysis." *Cultural Critique* 72, 36–75.

Fermi E., 1897. *Criminal Sociology.* New York: Appleton and Company.

Foucault M., 2003. *Abnormal: Lectures at the College de France, 1974–1975.* Trans. G. Burchell. New York: Picador.

Gamson W., 1995. "Hiroshima, The Holocaust, and the Politics of Exclusion." *American Sociological Review* 60, 1–20.

Garfinkel H., 1956. "Conditions of Successful Degradation Ceremonies." *American Sociological Review* 61, 420–424.

Garland D., 1990. *Punishment and Modern Society.* Chicago: University of Chicago Press.

Garvey S.P., 1999. "Punishment as Atonement." *UCLA Law Review,* 46, pp. 1801–1858.

—— 2000. "The Emotional Economy of Capital Sentencing." *New York University Law Review,* 75, 26–73.

Georget E., 1826. *Discussions medico-legale pour Henriette Cornier.* Paris: Migneret.

Givelber D., 2000. "Punishing Protestations of Innocence: Denying Responsibility and its Consequences." 37 *American Criminal Law Review,* 1363–1408.

Glaberson W., 2010. "Two Portraits of Triple Killer, Offered to Jurors, are at Odds." *New York Times,* October 29, A24.

Gobodo-Madikizela P., 2002. "Remorse, Forgiveness, and Rehumanization: Stories from South Africa." 42 *Journal of Humanistic Psychology,* 7–33.

—— 2003. *A Human Being Died That Night: A South African Story of Forgiveness.* New York: Houghton–Miflin.

Goffman E., 1961. *Asylums: Essays on the Social Situation of Mental Patients and Other Inmates.* New York: Doubleday Anchor.

—— 1971. *Relations in Public: Microstudies in Public Order.* New York: Basic Books.

Haney C., 1997. "Violence and the Capital Jury: Mechanisms of Moral Disengagement and the Impulse to Condemn to Death." *Stanford Law Review* 49, 1447–1486.

Hare R.D., 1996. "Psychopathy and Antisocial Personality Disorder: A case of Diagnostic Confusion." *Psychiatric Times,* 13 (2), 1–4, e-journal at <http://www.psychiatrictimes.com/p960239.html>

—— 1998. "Psychopathy, Affect, and Behavior." In David J. Cooke et al, *Psychopathy: Theory, Research, and Implications for Society.* Norwell, Mass: Kluwer Academic Publications, pp. 105–124.

—— 1999. *Without Conscience: The Disturbing World of the Psychopaths Among Us.* New York: Guilford Press.

Harris G.T., Rice M.E. and Cromier C.A., 1991. "Psychopathy and Violent Recidivism." *Law and Human Behavior* 15, no. 6, 625–637.

Harris M., 1990. *Justice Denied: The Law versus Donald Marshall.* Toronto: HarperCollins.

—— 1996. *The Judas Kiss.* Toronto: McClelland and Stewart.

Hay D., 1975. "Property, Authority, and the Criminal Law," in Douglas Hay et al, eds, *Albion's Fatal Tree.* Hammondsworth: Allen Lane, 17–63.

Henderson H., 2007. "Latimer only concerned about ending his own pain." *Toronto Star,* December 7, L4.

Herbeck D. and Michel L., 2001. "Death of a Terrorist Last Rites Renew Issue of Remorse." *Buffalo News,* A1.

Hickman A.T., Chief Justice and Chairman, 1989. *Royal Commission the Donald Marshall Jr. Prosecution, Vol. 1: Findings and Recommendations.* Halifax, N.S.: Queen's Printer.

Hochschild A., 2003. *The Commercialization of Intimate Life: Notes from Home and Work.* Berkeley: University of California Press.

Humphrey M., 2003. "From Victim to Victimhood: Truth Commissions and Trials as Rituals of Political Transition and Individual Healing." *Australian Journal of Anthropology,* 14 (2), 171–187.

Hunt J., 1985. "Police Accounts of Normal Force." *Journal of Contemporary Ethnography* 13, no. 4, 315–341.

Hunt J. and Manning P., 1991. "The Social Context of Police Lying." *Symbolic Interaction,* 14, no. 1, 51–70.

Hunter J., 2007. "Latimer: 'I still don't feel guilty." *Globe and Mail,* December 6, A10.

Huppke R., 2001. "McVeigh Executed for Oklahoma Site Bombing: Dies With No Trace of Remorse." *Associated Press Newswire.*

Jenish D., 1994. "What Would You Do?" *Maclean's Magazine,* November 28, 22.

Johnson D.T., 2002. *The Japanese Way of Justice: Prosecuting Crime in Japan.* New York: Oxford University Press.

Kadri S., 2005. *The Trial: from Socrates to O.J. Simpson.* New York: Random House.

Kaiser A., 2001. "Latimer: Something Ominous is Happening in the World of Disabled People." *Osgoode Hall Law Journal,* 39, 555–588.

Kari S., 2009. "Jury not told teen allegedly wanted 9 dead: Defendant pushed boyfriend to kill: Crown." *National Post,* March 19, A6.

Karp C. and Rosner C., 1991. *When Justice Fails: The David Milgaard Story.* Toronto: McClelland Stewart.

Kelsall T., 2005. "Truth, Lies, and Ritual: Preliminary Reflections on the Truth and Reconciliation Commission in Sierra Leone." *Human Rights Quarterly* 27, 361–391.

Kilty J., 2010. "Gendering violence, remorse, and the role of restorative justice: deconstructing public perceptions of Kelly Ellard and Warren Glotawski." *Contemporary Justice Review,* 13, no. 2, 155–172.

Kobil D.T., 2007. "Should Mercy Have a Place in Clemency Decisions," in Austin Sarat and Nassar Hussain, *Forgiveness, Mercy, and Clemency.* Stanford: Stanford University Press.

Komter M., 1998. *Dilemmas in the Courtroom: A Study of the trials of violent crime in the Netherlands.* N.J.: Erlbaum Associates.

Koonz C., 2003. *The Nazi Conscience.* Cambridge: Harvard University Press.

Krafft-Ebing R. von, 1905. *Textbook of Insanity, Based on Clinical Observations.* Transl. C.G. Craddock. Phila.: F.A. Davis Company.

Krog A. 2000. *Country of My Skull.* New York: Three Rivers Press.

Lamb S. 2003. "Symposium: Responsibility and Blame: Psychological and Legal Perspectives." *Brooklyn Law Review,* 929–959.

Lesser W., 1993. *Pictures at an Execution.* Cambridge, Mass.: Harvard University Press.

Lowry B. 1992. *Crossed Over: A Murder, A Memoir.* New York: Alfred A. Knopf.

Makin K., 2001. "Man jailed 29 years had alibi but police buried it." *Globe and Mail,* November 8: A1.

—— 2008. "Baltovich Goes Free." *Globe and Mail,* April 22, 1.

—— 2009. "Case puts focus on justice system's 'dirty little secret'". *Globe and Mail,* January 14, A7.

—— 2009. "Mother wrongly convicted in infant's death acquitted." *Globe and Mail,* December 8, A11.

Martel J., 2010. "Remorse and the Production of Truth." *Punishment and Society* 12, no. 4, 414–437.

Maruna S. and Copes H., 2005. "What Have We Learned from Five Decades of Neutralization Research?" *Crime and Justice* 32: 221–271.

Medwed D.S., 2008. "The Innocent Prisoner's Dilemma: Consequences of Failing to Admit Guilt at Parole Hearings." *Iowa Law Review* 93, 491–557.

Meloy J.R, 2004. *The Psychopathic Mind: Origins, Dynamics, and Treatment.* New York: Rowman and Littlefield

Meyer L.R., 2005. "Eternal Remorse." *Studies in Law, Politics, and Society,* 36, 139–154.

Miller W.I., 1998. *The Anatomy of Disgust.* Cambridge, Mass: Harvard University Press.

Millon T., with Davis R.D., 1996. *Disorders of Personality, DSM-IV and Beyond,* 2nd edition. New York: John Wiley and Sons.

Mitchell G.G., 2001. "'No Joy in this for Anyone' Reflections on the Exercise of Prosecutorial Discretion." *Sask. Law Review* 64, 491–510.

Moon C., 2009. *Narrating Political Reconciliation.* Plymouth, England: Lexington Books.

Morris A., 2002. "Shame, Guilt, and Remorse: Experiences from Family Group Conferences in New Zealand." In Ido Weijers and Antony Duff, eds, *Punishing Juveniles: Principle and Critique.* Portland, Oregon; Hart Publishing Company, 157–178.

Murphy J., 2007. "Remorse, Apology, and Mercy." *Ohio J. of Criminal Law,* 4, 423–454.

— — "Nebraska Bill Would Give Sum to Wrongly Convicted," January 25, 2009. *New York Times,* p. 25.

Nizer L., 1966. *The Jury Returns.* Doubleday: Garden City, New York.

Nussbaum M.C., 2004. *Hiding From Humanity: Disgust, Shame, and the Law.* Princeton, New Jersey: Princeton University Press.

O'Hear M., 1997. "Remorse, cooperation, and 'acceptance of responsibility': the structure, implementation, and reform of Section 3E1.1 of the Federal Sentencing Guidelines." *Northwestern University Law Review* 91, 1507–1573.

— — 2010. "Appelate Review of Sentences: Reconsidering Differences." *William and Mary L. Review,* 51, 2123–2168.

Paris E., 2001. *Long Shadows: Truth, Lies, and History.* Toronto: Vintage Canada.

Pauw J., 1996, Producer. *Prime Evil.* Documentary–SABC.

— — 1997. *Into the Heart of Darkness: Confessions of Apartheid's Assassins.* Johannesburg: Jonathan Ball Publishers.

— — 2006. *Dances with Devils: A Journalist's Search for Truth.* Cape Town, Zebra Press.

Payne L., 2008. *Unsettling Accounts: Neither Truth Nor Reconciliation in Confessions of State Violence.* Durham: Duke University Press.

Petrunik, M. and Weisman R., 2005. "Constructing Joseph Fredericks: Competing Narratives of a child sex murderer." *International Journal of Law and Psychiatry* 28, 75–96.

Plato, *Apology,* transl. Benjamin Jowett, 1892. eBook Collection.

Posel D. 2008. "History as Confession: The Case of the South African Truth and Reconciliation Commission." *Popular Culture,* 20 (1), 119–141.

Prichard J.C., 1842. *On the Different Forms of insanity in Relation to Jurisprudence.* London: Hippolyte Balliere.

Proeve M. and Tudor S., 2010. *Remorse: Psychological and Jurisprudential Perspectives.* Farnham, England: Ashgate.

Rafter N., 2004. "The Unrepentant Horse-Slasher: Moral Insanity and the Origins of Criminological Thought." *Criminology* 42, 979–1007.

Ray I., 1838. *Treatise on the Medical Jurisprudence of Insanity.* Boston: Charles C. Little and James Brown.

Reid F. and Hoffman D., Directors, 2000. *Long Night's Journey into Day* (film documentary). Iris Film/Iris Feminist Collective.

— — *Report of the Metropolitan Commissioners in Lunacy,* 1844. London.

Rippa S.A., 1992. *Education in a Free Society: An American History,* 7th edition, New York: Longman.

Roach K., 2001. "Crime and Punishment in the Latimer Case." *Sask. Law Review,* 64, 469–490.

Romano L., 2001. "Without Remorse McVeigh Put to Death." *Virginia Pilot and the Ledger–Star,* June 12, A11.

Ross M., 2004. *Why I Chose Death Rather than Fight for Life* at <http://www.ccadp.org/michaelross-whyichoose.htm> Last visited on October 25, 2012.

Sarat A., 1993. "Speaking of Death: Narratives of Violence in Capital Trials." *Law and Society Review* 27, 19–58.

— — 1999. "Remorse, Responsibility, and Criminal Punishment: an Analysis of Popular Culture." In Susan Bandes, ed., *Passions of the Law,* 168–190. New York: New York University Press.

Schafer A., 2007. "Justice Denied: Latimer case exposes flaws in legal system." *Winnipeg Free Press,* December 7, p. A7.

Scheff T., 2000. "Shame and the Social Bond: A Sociological Theory." *Sociological Theory* 18, 84–99.

Sereny G., 1995. *Albert Speer: His Battle with the Truth.* New York: The Haworth Press.

Shatan C.F., 1973. "The Grief of Soldiers: Vietnam Combat Veterans' Self-Help Movement." *The American Journal of Orthopsychiatry* 43 no. 4, 640–653.

Sher J., 2001. *"Until You Are Dead": Steven Truscott's Long Ride into History.* Toronto: Alfred A. Knopf Canada.

Stern E.M., ed., 1989. *Psychotherapy and the Remorseful Patient.* London: Routledge Press.

Stout M., 2005. *The Sociopath Next Door: The Ruthless Versus The Rest Of Us.* New York: Broadway Books.

Strange C., ed., 1996. *Qualities of Mercy: Justice, Punishment, and Discretion.* Vancouver: UBC Press.

Sundby S., 2005. *A Life and Death Decision: A Jury Weighs the Death Penalty.* New York: Palgrave Macmillan.

— — 1998. "The Capital Jury and Absolution: The Intersection of Trial Strategy, Remorse, and the Death Penalty." *Cornell L.R.,* 83, 1557–1598.

Sykes G. and Matza D. 1957. "Techniques of Neutralization: A Theory of Delinquency." *American Sociological Review* 22. 664–670.

Tavuchis N., 1991. *Mea Culpa: A Sociology of Apology and Reconciliation.* Stanford, Cal.: Stanford University Press.

Taylor G. 1985. *Pride, Shame, and Guilt.* New York: Oxford Press.

— — *Truth and Reconciliation Commission of South Africa Report,* Vol. 1–5, 2000. Cape Town: Truth and Reconciliation Commission.

Tudor S., 2001. *Compassion and Remorse: Acknowledging the Suffering Other.* Leuven: Peeters.

— — 2008. "Why Should Remorse be a Mitigating Factor in Sentencing?" *Criminal Law and Philosophy* 2, no. 3, 241–257.

Turner J., 1999. "From Apocalypse Now to Scotland the Brave." *Mail and Guardian Online at* <http://mg.co.za/article/1999-05-28-eugene-from-apocalypse-now-to-scotland-the> Last visited on January 19, 2013.

Tutu D., 1999. *No Future Without Forgiveness.* London: Rider Books

Vartkessian E.S., 2011. "Dangerously Biased: How Texas Capital Sentencing Statute Encourages Jurors to be Unreceptive to Mitigating Evidence." *Quinnipiac Law Review,* 29, 237–288.

Ward B., 2006. "Sentencing Without Remorse." *Loyola U. Chicago Law Journal* 38, 137–167.

Weingartner J.J., 1989. "Massacre at Biscari: Patton and American War Crime." *The Historian,* Vol. 1 (ii), no.2, 28–54.

Weisman R., 2004. "Showing Remorse: The Gap Between Expression and Attribution in Cases of Wrongful Conviction." *Canadian Journal of Criminal Justice* 46 (2): 121-38.

— — 2006. "Showing Remorse at the TRC: Towards a Constitutive Approach to Reparative Justice." *University of Windsor Annual Review—Access to Justice,* 24, no. 2, 221–239.

— — 2008. "Remorse and Psychopathy at the Penalty Phase of the Capital Trial: How Psychiatry's View of 'Moral Insanity' Helps Build the Case for Death." *Studies in Law, Politics, and Society,* 41, 187–217.

— — 2009. "Being and Doing: The Judicial Use of Remorse to Construct Character and Community." *Social and Legal Studies,* 18, no. 1, 47–69.

— — 2009. "Coupling and Decoupling Remorse and Forgiveness in Legal Discourse." In *Forgiveness: Promise, Possibility, and Failure,* Geoffrey Karabin and Karolina Wigura, co-editors—e-book at <https://www.interdisciplinarypress.net/online-store/ebooks/ethos-and-modern-life/forgiveness-promise-possibility-and-failure> Inter-Disciplinary Press.

Wood L.A. and McMartin C., 2007. "Constructing Remorse: Judge's Sentencing Decisions in Child Sexual Assault." *Journal of Language and Social Psychology,* 26, no. 4, 343–362.

Yardley W., May 14, 2005. "Execution in Connecticut: Final Day: One View of Killer's Execution; 'It was just a cowardly exit.'" *New York Times,* 1.

Young N., 2008. *I was Wrong: The Meaning of Apologies.* Cambridge: Cambridge University Press.

Zinger I., 2012. "Conditional Human Rights and Canada." *Canadian Journal of Criminology and Criminal Justice,* 54 (1), pp. 117–135.

Part III

Canadian Cases

Law Society of British Columbia v. Hanson [2004] A.C.W.S.J., Lexis 4716.

Manitoba and M.G.E.U. (Mytz) (Re) [2003] 121 L.A.C. (4th) 97.

Orca Bay Sports and Entertainment and Hotel, Restaurant, and Culinary Employees and Bartender Union (2002) B.C.P.L.A.J., 902.

P. (D.M.) (Re) [1989] O.J., 1574.

Quality Meat Packer Ltd and U.F.C.W. Local 175/633 [2002] Ontario C.L.A.S.J.

R. v. Bagshaw [2009], Superior Ct. of Ontario, O.J. 4123.

R. v. C. (V.) [2002] W.C.B.J., Lexis 862.

R. v. Cairns [2004] W.C.B.J., Lexis 3160

R. v. Callaghan [2003] N.S.C., Lexis 350.

R. v. Chisholm [2002] W.C.B.J., Lexis 175.

R. v. Clarke [2002] B.C.J. No. 1788, Lexis 4303,

R. v. Cooper [2002] N.J., No. 351, Lexis 456.

R. v. Cromien (T.) [2001] O.T.C., Lexis 2173.

R. v. Cromien (T.) [2002] O.A.C., Lexis 72.

R. v. D.A. [2004].

R. v. D.B.B. [2004] O.J. No. 1395 Lexis 1404

　R. v. E.M.S. [2003] On. C. Lexis 110.

R. v. La Fantaisie [2004] AB.C. Lexis 696.

R .v Galloway [2004] Sask. C.A., 187 C.C.C. (3rd) 305.

R. v. Gratton [2003] A.J. No. 1327 Lexis 109

R. v. Kaserbauer [2003] M. Ct. Q.B., Lexis 204

R. v. Lam [2004] AJ Lexis 112

R. v. Latimer [1994] Sask. Ct. of Appeal, S.J. No.630.

R. v. Latimer [1995] Sask. Ct. of Appeal, S.J. No. 402.

R. v. Latimer [1997] Sask. Ct. Of Queen's Bench, 121 C.C.C.(3rd) 326.

R. v. Latimer [2001] 1 SCR 3.

R. v. MacAdam [2003] P.E.I.S.C. 171 C.C.C. (3rd) 449.

R. v. McBride [2003] W.C.B.J. LEXIS 2833.

R. v. Pellizzon [2003] A.J.Lexis 1433.

R. v. P.(B.W.) [2003] W.C.B.J., Lexis 1720.

R. v. S. (M.) [2003] Sask C.A., 173 C.C.C. (3rd) 526.

R. v. Shore [2002] W.C.B.J. LEXIS 791.

R. v. T.E. [2003] B.C.J. No. 2512, Lexis 4587.

R. v. Todorovic [2009] Superior Court of Ontario, O.J., No.. 3246.

R. v. W.G.F. [2003] O.J. No. 1145 Lexis 3256.

Re Accuride Canada Inc. and C.A.W., Canada, Local 27 [2004] C.L.A.S.J. Lexis 255.

Re Brewers Distribution Ltd. and Distillery Workers Union, Local 300 [2003] C.L.A.S.J., Lexis 1464.

Re Meadow Park (London) and CAW Local 302 [2003] 122 L.A.C. (4th) 430.

U.S. Cases

Atkins v. Virginia [2002] 122 S.Ct. 2242.

Bronshtein v. Horn [2005] 404 F. 3rd 700 (3rd Cir.).

Bucklew v. Luebber [2006] 436 F. 3rd 1010 (8th Cir. 2006).

Cooper v. State [2003] 856 So. 2nd 969 (Fla.).

David Riggins, Petitioner v. State of Nevada, Respondent [1990] U.S. Briefs 8466.

Estelle, Corrections Director v. Smith [1981] S. Ct.. U.S. 454.

Harris v. Vazquez [1990] 913 F. 2nd 606 (9th Cir.).

Howard Ault, Appellant v. State of Florida, Appellee [2010] Supreme Ct. of Florida, FLA Lexis 1631.

Kimbrough v. State of Florida [2004] 886 So. 2nd 965, Lexis 958.

Lucero v. State of Texas [2008] Texas Criminal Appeal 219.

People v. Boyette [2002] 29 Cal. 4th 381.

People v. Crittenden [1994] 9 Cal. 4th 83.

People v. Davenport [1985] 41 Cal. 3rd 247.

People v. Farnham [2002] 28 Cal. 4th 107.

People v. Jurado [2006] 38 Cal. 4th 72.

People v. Marshall [1990] 50 Cal. 3rd 907.

People v. Mulero [1997] 176 I (ll) 2nd 444.

People v. Pollock [2004] 32 Cal. 4th 1153.

People v. Sakarias [2000] 22 Cal. 4th 596.

People v. Zambrano [2008] 41 Cal. 4th 1082.

Raby v. Dretke [2003] 78 Fed. Appx. 324 (5th Cir.)

Riggins v. Nevada [1992] 112 S.Ct. 1810.

Shelton v. State [1999] 744 A. 2nd 465 (Del.).

Sims v. Brown [2005] U.S. App. LEXIS 26806 (9th Cir.)

Smith v. Estelle [1979] U.S. Ct. of Appeal, 602 F. 2nd , 694.

State v. Campbell [2002] 95 Ohio St. 3rd 48.

State v. Daniels [1994] 337 N.C. 243.

State v. Bey [1999] Supreme Ct. of New Jersey, 736 A. 2nd 469.

State v. DiFrisco [2002] 174 N.J. 195.

State v. Ross [2004] 269 Conn. 213.

State v. Stephenson, 2005 Tenn. Crim. App. LEXIS 208.

State of New Jersey v. Wakefield [2008] 190 N.J. 397.

State of Washington v. Yates [2007] 161 Wn. 2nd 714.

United States v. McIlrath [2008] Ct. of Appeal (7 Circuit).

United States v. Williams [2010] U.S. District Ct. for the District of Hawaii, Lexis 79300.

United States of America, Appellee v. Michael Whitten et al [2010] 2nd Circuit, 610 F. 3rd, 168.

Westlaw (1997) 312609 (D. Col. Trans.) Transcription of Prosecutor's Address to Jury in trial of Timothy McVeigh.

Index

Name Index

Printed in Great Britain
by Amazon

64094329R00093